EQUALITY POSTPONED

Continuing Barriers to Higher Education in the 1980s

Report from a Policy Conference on
Postsecondary Programs for the Disadvantaged,
held at Wingspread, Racine, Wisconsin, in June 1982

Stephen H. Adolphus, editor

College Entrance Examination Board, New York, 1984

Printed in the United States of America.

Copies of this book may be ordered from College Board Publications, Box 886, New York, New York 10101. The price is $12.95.

Editorial inquiries concerning this book should be directed to: Editorial Office, The College Board, 888 Seventh Avenue, New York, New York 10106.

Library of Congress Catalog Card Number: 84-45728

ISBN No. 0-87447-188-5

Contents

National Advisory Committee

Stephen H. Adolphus
Chief
Bureau of Higher Education Opportunity Programs
New York State Education Department

Patrick N. Callan
Director
California Postsecondary Education Commission

Gilberto de los Santos
Dean of Students and Instructional Services
Pan American University

Rupert A. Jemmott
Executive Director
Educational Opportunity Fund
New Jersey Department of Higher Education

Conrad Jones
Assistant Vice President
Office of Affirmative Action
Temple University

Velma Monteiro-Williams
Program Manager
FIPSE/MISIP Program
United States Department of Education

Alfred L. Moyé
Vice President for Academic Affairs and Dean of Faculties
Roosevelt University

Staff
Theresa Czapary
Conference Coordinator/Research Assistant

The Policy Statement

of the 1982 Wingspread Conference on Postsecondary Programs for the Disadvantaged

We believe that the American promise to enable each person to become all he or she is capable of being will be met *only* if all means for personal development are equally available to all people, regardless of circumstances or background. While we recognize that progress has been made toward achieving greater access for minority and disadvantaged populations, they are still severely underrepresented at all levels of postsecondary education. Furthermore, this country's position in the family of nations can be maintained only if it realizes the development of all people to their full potential, particularly those from groups that have been historically excluded from higher education.

The conference places special emphasis on the need for:

- Quality education for all, including minority and disadvantaged students.

- Recognition of the interrelatedness of all levels of education, since efforts that improve achievement at the elementary and secondary levels increase the likelihood of success at the postsecondary level.

- State and federal action in cooperation with postsecondary institutions to overcome the underrepresentation of minority students in many career areas and particularly at the postgraduate level and in the more prestigious and highly selective courses of study.

- Recognition of the experiences and effectiveness of postsecondary opportunity programs for minorities and the disadvantaged.

- Political action on the part of the education community to respond to the fiscal and social crises threatening equal educational opportunity.

The Need for Quality

Wingspread participants recommend the following positions relating to quality.

1. Equal educational opportunity for minorities and the disadvantaged must be interpreted as an equal opportunity for *quality* education. We define quality as excellence in academic preparation at all levels, soundly based in the essential disciplines, for graduation from secondary, undergraduate, and postgraduate institutions.

2. The quality of an educational institution is determined by a mix of factors having to do with faculty, resources, and students. However, the most important quality indicator for an institution must be its success in ensuring that it educates students to meet performance standards that enable them to function effectively in the next steps in their education and their careers, and not the level of preparation of the students it admits.

3. The value of institutions in providing opportunity to minorities and the disadvantaged must be measured by the extent to which they educate students while helping to satisfy their social and physiological needs, without compromising appropriate exit standards.

These positions follow from a recognition that public dissatisfaction with the state of the economy, social changes over the last decade, and disenchantment with educational effectiveness at all levels have led to calls for higher standards of educational quality. We are also concerned that some institutions have not clearly defined quality or have compromised on quality in programs serving disadvantaged or minority students. For this reason, we reemphasize that equal educational opportunity for minorities and the disadvantaged must be interpreted as an equal opportunity for *quality*. The quality of special programs for disadvantaged and minority students should be judged by how effectively such programs contribute to the overall accomplishment of institutional goals.

These new understandings are imperative as this nation considers the future of equal educational opportunities for minorities and the disadvantaged. While acknowledging that many students leave secondary schools unprepared for further education, we caution postsecondary institutions against attempting to assure quality by raising admissions standards without making alternative provisions for admitting less-well-prepared students who need or can benefit from postsecondary education. Postsecondary institutions must recognize that additional time and resources must be provided to achieve the new definiton of quality postsecondary education for all—most important, for those students who are now receiving inadequate preparation at the elementary and secondary levels.

The Interrelatedness of Elementary, Secondary, and Postsecondary Education

For too long education has been segmented into elementary, secondary, and postsecondary levels with little articulation among the levels. Regarding the interrelatedness of all levels of education, we recommend the following positions.

4. Higher education institutions have a particular responsibility to improve the preparation and training of students who will become elementary and secondary school teachers, especially those who will be teachers of minority and disadvantaged students.

5. Elementary and secondary schools must strengthen curriculums and instruction in all disciplines, and concomitantly raise their expectations for performance, so that all students, in particular minority and disadvantaged students, can develop the appropriate competencies for transition to post-secondary education.

Success or failure at one level of education inevitably surfaces at another. For example, deficiencies in the preparation of elementary school teachers, if not corrected, will contribute to low levels of pupil performance in elementary school classes—a condition that will follow these students through junior and senior high school, and, for those who remain in the system, into college and university work. Looked at another way, practices that discriminate against the poor and minorities in elementary and secondary education produce a need for postsecondary programs that address the underpreparation of those who are disadvantaged as a result of such practices. We need to examine and evaluate the present condition of elementary and secondary schools, including the preparation of their personnel and the outcomes of their practices and processes. To the extent that these schools are successful in elevating achievement, the success of their graduates in higher education will be improved.

6. We urge state and local boards of education to take the following actions.

- Set goals for high achievement by *all* students in reading, writing, and mathematics.
- Establish management and instructional routines for attaining these goals.
- Monitor these routines regularly to assess goal achievement.
- Urge principals and faculties in schools with low-income and minority students to set high expectations for those students' academic success and to act on the belief that such students can perform at high levels and meet rigorous high school graduation standards.

- Reaffirm principals' responsibility for creating a school climate that is conducive to learning and for ensuring student compliance with clear rules and regulations.
- Encourage principals to assist teachers to develop strategies and concepts that lead to high student achievement.
- Reaffirm teachers' responsibility for successful teaching.
- Set graduation requirements in mathematics and scientific literacy at a level that will enable graduates to be successful in college and other endeavors requiring such skills and competencies.
- Review the high school curriculums in history, civics, art, music, literature, expression, drama, poetry, and speech so that the contributions of all cultures in America are incorporated—not as an appendage to European culture, but as significant in their own right.
- Provide bilingual instruction, including instruction in content areas, in the students' native languages.
- Orient high school instruction more toward achieving competency and skill mastery rather than subject-matter mastery.
- Allot more time to instructional activities, and eliminate routines that diminish this time.

School administrators, teachers, and other staff must be better prepared to meet the needs of the disadvantaged and minorities for quality elementary and secondary education. The role of schools of education in providing such preparation is critical.

Governmental Action

The conference participants make the following statement about the problem of underrepresentation of minorities in important career areas.

7. We note the low percentage of minorities pursuing education in fields based in mathematics and science, and the scarcity of minority graduates with advanced degrees, notably doctoral and law degrees. Equal opportunity education demands that institutions make special efforts to encourage and to prepare minority students to enter careers in which they have been traditionally underrepresented, many of which represent areas of high national need. We recommend state and federal actions in cooperation with postsecondary institutions to overcome this deficiency.

Graduate and professional education for the disadvantaged and minorities is a very high priority because of past neglect and present severe underrepresentation. We call for strengthened state and federal efforts that ensure more blacks, Hispanics, and Native Americans complete advanced degrees, including M.D.s and Ph.D.s in the arts and humanities, computer sciences, education, engineering, life sciences, mathematics, physical sciences, and the social sciences. Low productivity in many of these fields is a problem of national concern.

8. We further propose the following specific governmental actions to combat the problem.

▪ State and federal legislation to encourage and stimulate graduate and professional institutions to develop and implement effective programs increasing minority enrollment, and to provide rewards for doing so.

▪ Commitment by state and federal governments to take specific steps to ensure that all their agencies recruit increasing numbers of qualified minority and disadvantaged people and to provide career development for those whom they employ.

▪ Critical examination by state and federal governments of policies and practices that may, either directly or indirectly, adversely affect or impede appropriate representation of the disadvantaged and minorities in fields requiring graduate or professional education.

▪ Commitment by state and federal governments to strengthen the role of traditionally black institutions, and of institutions predominantly serving ethnic minority groups, in preparing their students for graduate and professional education.

▪ Commitment by appropriate agencies and organizations to strengthen the role of other undergraduate institutions in preparing the disadvantaged and minorities for graduate and professional education.

Although these recommendations for specific action are addressed to state and federal governments for the most part, we understand that people in education institutions and in communities, committed to the ideal of fuller representation of the disadvantaged and minorities, must work diligently, forcefully, and continuously for its achievement. The disadvantaged and minorities must acquire genuinely effective intellectual and professional skills. If they fail to do so, the national ideals of equality and responsibility are hollow. Effective enabling legislation is essential, as are the efforts of people of good will.

Proven Strategies

The experiences of postsecondary opportunity programs for the disadvantaged and minorities have yielded numerous concrete strategies and results. We recommend the following policies and practices.

9. The effectiveness of postsecondary opportunity programs for the disadvantaged and minorities must be recognized. Such programs have effected some of the most significant improvements in postsecondary education of the last two decades by promoting access and by helping students who might otherwise not have had the benefits of a college education to

satisfy academic standards of success. They have also provided advocacy and role models for students. We recommend continuing and strengthening such programs.

10. The experiences of postsecondary opportunity programs for the disadvantaged and minorities suggest that successful programs have a number of common elements. These include:

- Strength and continuity of program administrative leadership.
- Staff and faculty expectations that students can succeed.
- Pre-semester and pre-college orientation.
- Adequately targeted remedial and developmental courses and appropriate recognition of successful completion of these courses.
- Accurate advice and information about selecting courses and professors and about transferability of credits.
- Concentration of special services at certain crucial times (i.e., first semester of freshman year and following transfer).
- Timely academic advisement and career counseling.
- Commitment to opportunity programs at the chief executive level.
- Articulation with secondary schools and between two- and four-year colleges.
- Clear outlining of services and expectations for students.
- Continuous monitoring and feedback of student progress.

All postsecondary programs are urged to incorporate these effective approaches.

11. We also urge all institutions of higher education to follow the example of postsecondary opportunity programs in treating all students with dignity, irrespective of their previous experiences, present qualifications, financial need, major, or need for special assistance. Positive ego reinforcement and acceptable self-image are facilitators of success.

The Political Agenda

We call on the higher education community for political action to respond to the crises threatening equal educational opportunity, including proposed governmental reductions in funding, increasingly restrictive admissions requirements, and reductions in minority enrollments. Political action for equal opportunity for quality education for disadvantaged and minority groups involves multiple levels: campus-based groups, community organizations, state and federal legislatures, and constituency and national educational organizations, acting both singly and in concert.

12. People in academic communities concerned with equal educational opportunity have an obligation to: inform and promote civic education; establish alliances with groups such as faculty, administrators, governing

boards, students, parents, alumni, and labor organizations; give expert testimony on issues relevant to the disadvantaged; and coalesce in professional and disciplinary organizations to mobilize their collective strength.

Conclusion

As we move toward a postindustrial society, the future of our nation will depend on the strength of our human resources. Investment in human capital to achieve the maximum educational development of all people therefore becomes our priority. Concerned people must promote and advocate financial aid entitlement programs, compensatory education services, institutional support programs, and all of those practices that enhance equal educational opportunity. Concerned people are not just people in the academic community. We must work to include parents, community organizations, and, especially, those who have already benefitted from participation in such programs. Minority educational constituency and disciplinary groups especially must give leadership to articulating progress or retrogression in higher education by calling attention to such indicators of institutional commitment as admissions and retention policies and results, hiring faculty and staff from underrepresented groups, appropriate curriculum, and adequate budget.

Until all of the least-advantaged groups are fully included in all levels of higher education, we have not attained the goal of equal educational opportunity. There is in the nation an inequitable distribution of minorities at the various levels and in the various disciplines and types of postsecondary education. The goal of equal opportunity for quality education will not have been realized until effective steps have been taken to remove all of the barriers that have excluded these groups.

The Policy Conference on Postsecondary Programs for the Disadvantaged Wingspread, Racine, Wisconsin, June, 1982

Preface

In 1970 the College Board convened a colloquium on Barriers to Higher Education at the Wingspread Conference Center, which examined the major barriers that at the time limited the equal access of minority and disadvantaged students to higher education. The participants at that conference were some of the key figures of the postsecondary opportunity movement. Much of their attention was devoted to the topics of admissions testing and the adequacy of student financial aid.

One of the key strategies that has evolved to attack these barriers in the years since the 1970 conference has been the establishment of postsecondary opportunity programs at the national, state, and institutional levels. These programs of broad-ranging academic, social, and fiscal support for minority and disadvantaged students were virtually nonexistent before 1970. Now they exist at most colleges and universities in the country and as such represent a large commitment of public and institutional resources.

We called the 1982 national Policy Conference on Postsecondary Programs for the Disadvantaged to look at the history of the last decade of opportunity programs, to evaluate their current circumstances, and to recommend policies for their future development. In the process we were able to see how far we have come and how far we still have to go.

The opportunity programs have evolved beyond a primary role in recruitment, admissions, and financial aid to a whole range of support services. Today many of these programs, having survived past the first years of haste in which they were established, are distinguished by careful attention to evaluation and documentation of results, planning, professional development of staff, fiscal responsibility, and skilled negotiating on behalf of student interests.

The results of the programs have been numerous. Gains have been made in achieving undergraduate racial integration. Success ratios for students in many postsecondary opportunity programs, measured in terms of persistence to graduation, approach or even exceed those of regularly admitted students. In addition, more broadly targeted programs of financial aid and developmental education now exist alongside the postsecondary opportunity programs, due in large part to the models first developed for special populations.

The need for the 1982 conference stemmed from a recognition that, despite these gains, large gaps still exist in achieving equity in higher education and that, in an atmosphere of fierce competition for public resources, these programs can anticipate pressures for self-examination and change.

The conference was supported by a grant from the federal Fund for the Improvement of Postsecondary Education (FIPSE) to the New York State Board of Regents. It was conducted with the assistance and cooperation of the Johnson Foundation and held at Wingspread, the foundation's headquarters in Racine, Wisconsin. The College Board, sponsor of the first conference and publisher of the resulting book, *Barriers to Higher Education,* contributed to the 1982 conference throughout by the active participation of several of its staff, by providing technical and editorial advice and assistance, and by providing the resources to publish this book.

A national advisory committee representing major geographic regions, agencies, and constituencies planned, guided, and organized the conference.

The 55 conference participants selected by the Advisory Committee in consultation with the Fund for the Improvement of Postsecondary Education included key policy makers and leaders in the field of education, with long-standing records of advocacy and research in the area of postsecondary educational opportunity. Four of the speakers at the 1970 colloquium, Alexander Astin, Edmund Gordon, George Hanford, and Stephen Wright, also participated and presented papers at the 1982 gathering.

The commissioned papers were designed to cover the ethical, political, academic, social, and fiscal dimensions of the subject of postsecondary equity. The major papers were paired with reaction papers by authors with somewhat different points of view.

Several individuals made special presentations. Carol Stoel, of the Fund for the Improvement of Postsecondary Education, described its general mission, special emphases, other projects of a similar nature, and its future concerns and interests. Stephen Wright introduced the conference by describing the linkages between the 1970 colloquium and the 1982 conference. George Hanford discussed the changing and somewhat unexpected new social and political barriers that have arisen partly as a consequence of the changes in educational access since 1970. Donald Henderson, who was the conference rapporteur, concluded the sessions with a description of the conference process from the perspective of personal and group interactions.

Edmund Gordon presented the first major conference paper on the subject of the Social and Ethical Context of Special Programs. His major conclusion was that opportunity programs have been denied an adequate opportunity to succeed by virtue of having been undercapitalized conceptually and financially. Frederick Humphries, in his response, agreed with the premise that opportunity programs have been denied adequate resources but disagreed somewhat on the lack of conceptual theories on serving disadvantaged populations. He contended that documented and effective theories and practices for meeting these needs are in existence but have not been incorporated into established educational knowledge because of elitist societal and educational practices.

James Rosser, in the paper on the Role of Government and the Public Sector, stated that postsecondary opportunity programs cannot afford to tie their future so closely to the policies of the federal government. He also proposed methods by which to strengthen programs and help insure their continued existence. In response, I argued that the federal government cannot be excused from fulfilling its responsibility to increase opportunities for equal educational access for all of its people.

Barbara Sizemore's paper, which dealt with the Connections between Postsecondary Programs for the Disadvantaged and Elementary and Secondary Education, called for high-quality education for all students, especially disadvantaged black students, and outlined specific steps for reorganizing and changing elementary and secondary schools to insure quality. Alex Sherriffs' response was in essential agreement with Sizemore's major conclusions and added observations and recommendations based on his experience in the California educational system.

Alfredo de los Santos's paper describes the special conditions and needs of Hispanic elementary and secondary students. This paper was commissioned at the conference to answer the need to balance Sizemore's paper, which deals primarily with black students.

Michael Olivas's paper, New Populations, New Arrangements, outlined his perceptions on declines in access, which he believes resulted from a changed public mood in addressing the problem and from governmental and other institutional barriers that continue to exist and to reinforce each other. In response, Alfred Moyé presented several recommendations for meeting the educational needs of a changing population, particularly the adult learner, in an increasingly complex and technological society.

Alexander Astin's presentation described the major findings and recommendations, with particular emphasis on the value-added concept, of the *Final Report of the Commission on Higher Education of Minorities.* This document, which was by fortunate coincidence prepared and available just prior to the conference, has now been incorporated in a larger overall study, *Minorities in American Higher Education.* Kenneth Ashworth challenged some of the assumptions of the value-added concept and added a different perspective on the mission and value of community colleges.

Following each presentation at the conference the participants discussed the major points with the presenters. The papers and the following large-group discussions served as a springboard for participants, who then met in smaller group sessions to draft statements and recommendations on several comprehensive topics. The resulting position papers were used in meetings of the Advisory Committee following the conference to develop the conference statement.

As Donald Henderson described in his presentation, the discussions and debates at the conference were consistently lively and provocative—and occasionally heated. The debates, which included substantial disagreements with the major points of some papers, served to clarify positions and to coalesce the participants. They were also used by some of the authors to refine and revise their papers following the conference. The result of the conference was not only the development of a tangible product, namely the policy statement of recommendations on future needs and directions for the education of minorities and the disadvantaged, but also the creation of a network of individuals committed to working for the ideal of expanding postsecondary equity.

Many individuals contributed to the success of the conference: the authors for preparing stimulating and informative papers; Robert Albright, Alfredo de los Santos, Richard Donovan, Manuel Gomez, and Joseph Harris, whose excellent facilitation helped to maintain the conference focus; Carol Stoel, who provided excellent advice and encouragement throughout; Dorothy Knoell, who assisted the Advisory Committee in its planning and organizing activities on several occasions; Diane Olsen for her editorial and technical advice and assistance; Henry Halsted, vice president of the Johnson Foundation, for the many courtesies and high level of amenities provided to all participants; Donald Henderson for his service as rapporteur; Alvin P. Lierheimer for permitting the undersigned project director the chance to take risks; and Theresa Czapary for her coordinating and other staff work.

Stephen H. Adolphus
Albany, New York

Editor's note:

There were really three formal aspects to the conference: the commissioned papers; the policy statement; and organized discussions, initially focused on the papers themselves, and subsequently on generic topics that became the basis for the policy statement. In addition, the presentations of some of the formal papers were immediately and spontaneously followed by intensive debate and discussion. The participants wanted to make sure that some of that discussion was captured in this report on the conference and were especially concerned that the reader be aware that the papers were prepared to elicit discussion—which they assuredly did—and not to represent a consensus on the part of the conference—which they assuredly did not; the policy statement performs that function. The occasional editor's notes reflect the tenor of the more heated discussions.—S.H.A.

Foreword

This publication is being prepared as the Fund for the Improvement of Post-secondary Education (FIPSE) enters its tenth year of operation. It is particularly fitting that these two events—the publication of these papers and the celebration of the Fund's tenth anniversary—should occur simultaneously. FIPSE was originally created, in part, to respond to the changing patterns of enrollments in higher education during the sixties and seventies, when larger numbers of adults, women, and minority students entered college, and much of its early work concerned projects designed to improve access to higher education opportunities for all students.

"National Project II: Beyond the Revolving Door," for example, was a FIPSE-sponsored project that permitted 10 colleges with exemplary programs for disadvantaged students to evaluate their work and to explore means of improving the services they provided. The basic objective of this program was to focus national attention on programs and strategies that had proved, demonstrated track records of success in working effectively with nontraditional college students. Programs that had been awarded grants in this competition examined their efforts at boosting student academic performance and in improving retention and graduation rates.

Concern with the academic achievement and retention rates of minority and disadvantaged students continues to dominate the priorities of equal opportunity programs. The quality of a program is frequently measured by the number of students who are retained each year and by the number who graduate. FIPSE has continued to fund programs seeking to improve the techniques for aiding students to adapt to the challenges of college-level academic work.

A notable program, for example, was created at the University of California at Berkeley, which since 1978 has been principally responsible for improved performance in mathematics and science courses by undergraduate minority students. The program—Professional Development Program (PDP)—organizes entering minority students into small study groups. These groups participate in workshops on problem solving in the sciences; group members attend the same classes, and they work together on the assigned classroom work. Members are taught to be responsible for each other's progress in class and for each other's general well-being. Achieving high standards of performance becomes part of one's commitment to oneself, to other members of the group, and to the program itself.

Retention rates for the students in the program are higher than those of white students, and PDP students outperform white students in precalculus and beginning calculus classes. Of critical significance have been attempts to disseminate the program's techniques for working with minority students. Two programs on other University of California campuses boast of similarly impressive retention and academic performance statistics.

PDP is by no means alone as an exemplary program created to serve the needs of minority disadvantaged students. After more than 10 years of operation we have come to learn a great deal about how to create and maintain successful programs. Just about the only technique that has not been perfected is the one that guarantees a steady, reliable source of funding to keep these programs alive.

Were we in an environment in which success was rewarded with adequate resources, equal opportunity programs would long ago have been freed from the annual anxiety and paranoia that attend the scramble for funding. A means would have been discovered long ago for standardizing and institutionalizing those techniques and practices that best promote the achievement of each learner's goals and aspirations. After more than 10 years of struggle, however, this conference finds us still attempting to convince the powers that be that providing all citizens with equal access to higher education opportunities is both desirable and possible. We are still trying to convince the skeptics that disadvantaged students can be given a quality education without lowering standards of academic excellence. And finally, we are still trying to convince the folk with the purse strings that an investment in the education of a disadvantaged youngster yields far greater returns to society than almost any other conceivable expenditure of funds.

The papers published in this volume represent an attempt to make this case yet another time. If the arguments for a continued role for equal opportunity programs in higher education seem somehow familiar, and if the calls for continued commitments to the goals of a more democratized system of American higher education appear to echo previous calls for such a commitment, we urge the reader to consider the source. FIPSE support for this conference is consistent with our mandate to find means of improving postsecondary education. In the past 10 years we have been pleased to have been associated with much that has been new and innovative, but this conference reminds us that not all improvements are the result of the creation of something new. An improvement often occurs because the crucial step is taken to accept a prototype that has proved itself under rigorous conditions to be "the real thing" and to move heaven and earth to support its continued acceptance and expansion.

Equal opportunity programs simply cannot continue to be treated as peripheral to the missions of the institutions that house and support them. The need that these programs were created to meet has not disappeared; rather, it has grown enormously. A means for responding to that need exists. All that is lacking is the will to match the need with adequate means for getting the job done. One clear consensus among conference participants is that the nation does not have another 10 years in which to make the decision.

Robert E. Fullilove, III
Carol F. Stoel
The Fund for the Improvement of Postsecondary Education

Introduction

Stephen J. Wright

Twelve years ago this very month, in this very place, the College Board conducted a national conference on barriers to higher education. The conference made the valid assumption that certain formidable barriers stood in the way of equal opportunity for the disadvantaged minorities of America and that if these barriers could be effectively analyzed and their enormous impact clearly delineated we could systematically address them and thereby either eliminate them or minimize their influence as impeding factors in the achievement of equal educational opportunities.

Now we knew at the outset that we could not consider all of the barriers. We therefore selected those that we believed to be the most critical at that time. The organization and structure of higher education was believed to be a barrier. The abuse of admissions tests was believed to be a barrier. Discriminatory admissions policies, a scarcity of effective support programs, and finally the lack of money—all were barriers. We then asked ourselves who, among the educators of the nation, could prepare the best analyses of the barriers and who could best prepare a critical response. The list we put together still reads like a Who's Who in American education: Alexander Astin, Helen Astin, Kenneth Clark, Humphrey Doermann, Edmund Gordon (who is here again with another paper), Timothy Healy, Hugh Lane, Winton Manning, John Millett, Julian Stanley, B. Alden Thresher, and Warren Willingham. We invited about 50 other influential educators from 20 states and the District of Columbia, and we spent three exciting days discussing— sometimes heatedly—those barriers and dozens of related problems.

The idea of that conference was, I think, an excellent one, and the papers presented were published as *Barriers to Higher Education,* a book that has been extensively quoted over the years in the educational literature. It would be a very great accomplishment if we could report 12 years later that the barriers to higher education of the nation's minorities had been removed or minimized to the point where equal educational opportunity in America was no longer a problem, but every informed individual knows that this is very far from the case.

Nevertheless, some substantial progress has been made, especially in the area of access. I cite this because it means that organized effort does indeed make a positive difference. But very serious problems of persistence through graduate and professional schools still remain—and this is not all. Reductions and threatened reductions in financial aid, declining support for higher education, rising tuition, cutbacks in enrollments in public institutions, and rising admissions standards, particularly in public institutions, are jeopardizing the progress that has been made. In times such as these, it is the powerless who get hurt first and who get hurt most seriously. In the face of these developments it is imperative that we keep reminding the nation of the critical importance of equal opportunity as a meaningful national goal. For the democratic foundation of this nation is built on the notion of equality of opportunity for its citizens, and there can be no such thing as equality of opportunity in the larger sense without equal *educational* opportunities. Horace Mann was right when he said more than a century ago that education is the great equalizer of the conditions of men.

Stephen Adolphus, chief of the Bureau of Higher Education Opportunity Programs of the New York State Department of Education, has seen the situation that I have just described emerging, and he has seen it with 20-20 vision. But he has done more than just see it and more than just view it with alarm. He has conceived this second Wingspread conference on the higher education of America's disadvantaged minorities as a policy conference on the postsecondary programs for the disadvantaged. As the conditions that brought these programs into existence are changing and financial support for them is dwindling, we have met to consider how the objectives of these programs may be pursued in the context of the 1980s. Steve not only formulated the theme of this second conference but successfully sought out the sources of financial support. In addition, he put together a distinguished list of presenters and reactors: George Hanford, president of the College Board; Jim Rosser, president of Cal State at Los Angeles; Michael Olivas, who is moving to head the Center of Law and Education at the University of Houston; Barbara Sizemore of the Black Studies Department of the University of Pittsburgh; Sandy Astin, president of the Higher Education Research Institute, Edmund Gordon, professor of psychology at Yale. I happen to know them all and have worked with them in some capacity over the years. Not only are their papers instructive, but these men and women bring to this conference splendid training, vast experience, and deep insight into the problems that we will be discussing. I know only two of the reactors, but if those two are in any sense representative of the others, they all belong in the same league as the presenters. For such leadership as this Steve has earned our deepest gratitude.

With such a setting as this, I hold high the hope that we who are privileged to participate in this conference will search our experience, our minds, and especially our imaginations and make the most of this splendid opportunity. I hope that as a result of our deliberations in this place, the objectives of the special programs will be vigorously pursued during the 1980s and the march toward equal educational opportunities will be accelerated.

Barriers to Higher Education Revisited

George H. Hanford

This conference has been convened to pursue the engineering of social change: in this instance, overcoming persistent barriers to equal opportunity for education.

I use the verb "pursue" because our gathering follows by a dozen years that earlier conference you have heard about. I use the adjective "persistent" because many barriers remain, despite real progress in the pursuit of equal opportunity in education.

I have chosen to emphasize the noun "change," for, as Steve Wright pointed out in his preface to the report of that earlier conference, it summarizes the sense of the discussions then.

The truth about change is, of course, that it occurs whether we will it or not—and, furthermore, that the changes that we seek to engineer here, like the changes we sought to engineer a dozen years ago, will inevitably bring unexpected outcomes in their wake.

Isaac Asimov makes the point this way: "The important thing to predict is not the automobile, but the parking problem; not the television, but the soap opera; not the income tax, but the expense account; not the bomb, but the arms race." Michael Olivas hints at the problem in his discussion of the reliance on federal legislation to change the educational system. But, more specifically, we have witnessed the phenomenon of unexpected outcomes in the field of education in our attack on the barriers to opportunity. And, because I know the College Board's part in the process best, let me make my point first and most concretely there—my point that the changes we talked about engineering here a dozen years ago have brought unexpected consequences.

In my judgment, the College Board can rightfully claim some small share of responsibility for two important changes over the last quarter-century:

first, the immense broadening of educational opportunity according to ability rather than social status, and second, the emergence of a philosophy, and the mechanisms, for providing assistance to those who might not otherwise be able to take advantage of their opportunity for economic reasons.

With respect to the first change, recognizing ability instead of status, the College Board was founded in 1900 with agreement on common college entrance requirements, given meaning by common written examinations to determine whether or not candidates had met those requirements. Half a century later, the Scholastic Aptitude Test (SAT) helped colleges broaden their search for talent to all parts of the country and to all kinds of preparatory settings. The goal of this then-new test was to open up access to higher education both vertically, in terms of ability, and geographically, in terms of mobility.

It was in large part the curriculum-free nature of the SAT that made such opening up possible. Especially in the 1950s and after, when the demand for places at college threatened to exceed (and for some selective colleges did exceed) capacity, the allocation of available spaces was made much fairer, at least in terms of those times. Yet, in retrospect, we now realize that the change we sought to engineer also planted the seed of an unexpected outcome—a consequence to which I will return in a moment.

With respect to the second change we sought to engineer here in 1970, lowering the financial barriers to higher education, it was, again, in that era after World War II that the nation's experience with the GI Bill proved what many educators already believed—that a much larger portion of the college-age population could make good use of a college education for their own benefit and society's, if they could only afford the cost. In this context the economic factor emerged as critical. Again, the College Board provided the medium for agreement—this time, on how to make it possible for students to make choices among colleges on educational rather than economic grounds through the College Scholarship Service.

To engineer this change, to achieve this goal, we helped to develop the concept of financial aid awarded on the basis of need. It is a concept that has led to a major commitment of public funds, not to institutions but to individuals. It is a concept that has enabled them to take advantage of opportunities that otherwise would not have been available to them and to make choices they otherwise would not have had.

Yet here, too, there was an unanticipated outcome—a second outcome we did not foresee.

What were the unanticipated outcomes of these two major changes in according educational opportunity?

In the case of the SAT it has been a blurring of the distinction between curriculum-free and schooling-free testing, and a consequent relaxation in academic standards in our secondary schools. The very fact that the test affords all students an opportunity to display developed academic abilities without demanding that they all pursue an identical course of study has led to the erroneous assumption that it does not matter what they study.

In the financial aid area, until the advent of the College Scholarship Service and the philosophy of need-based aid that it represents, scholarships meant dollars for brains. One unexpected consequence of changing the emphasis to need has been a de-emphasis on the competitive element of academic achievement.

And there was a second consequence: the political attractiveness of providing such aid from public sources—yes, as well as the social wisdom of helping a larger proportion of able young men and women maximize their abilities—has extended the concept of aid from one of student need to what some would deride as family subsidy.

These developments have exposed the entire structure of public support for student financial aid to criticism and to not always carefully differentiated attacks.

Could we have foreseen these consequences? Perhaps. If we had, should we have tried to avoid them? Of course. Should the possibility that something like them would emerge have prevented us from pursuing the goals we sought? Emphatically not! For, however much hindsight shows that we might have done better, I do not believe that these unanticipated consequences in any degree outweigh the tremendous good that has been accomplished by the changes we engineered—the very changes that contributed to their emergence.

Progress has been made, and times have changed. Now new challenges confront us—challenges in part the consequence of the progress we have made. In these new circumstances the College Board is once again turning its attention to the question of quality of academic preparation for college, just as it did at the beginning of this century.

Similarly, we are wary of sweeping solutions to the unanticipated and unwanted consequences of the revolution in financial aid. We tend to believe that determining satisfactory academic performance as a condition of continued aid should be an institutional prerogative, suited to the particular student body and instructional mission of the institution. By the same token, we do not defend aid that is need-based in name only and goes to those who are not in need as well. I do not mean to suggest that the College Board is dismissing the need for extensive and careful discussion and consideration of those issues—for here, too, we must be wary of the unexpected outcomes that might be generated.

That is why we are involved in our Educational EQuality Project, a 10-

year effort to improve the quality of preparation for college in the secondary schools. But our approach today is quite different. In 1900 the colleges set forth their requirements, and the schools were expected to do whatever was needed to prepare students to meet them.

Today through our EQuality project, we seek to do two things: first, to help break down Alex Sherriffs's "barriers between the nation's colleges and schools" and to bring school and college people together to agree on the standards of preparation young people should have to succeed in college, and, second, to find ways of providing that preparation to all students who seek it. For together school and college people must persuade the larger society not only that such standards are essential to its future health, but also that society must provide the support, both moral and material, for the pursuit of those standards. And, most important they . . . you . . . we must persuade the larger society that the support must be provided in ways that will enable the maximum number of students— including minority and disadvantaged youth—to meet those standards. We must, because we know that the danger—a consequence that can be anticipated and avoided—is that a re-emphasis on quality through selectivity, rather than quality through enablement, will lessen the emphasis on equality of opportunity that we continue to hold as an all-important, essential objective.

It is tempting to describe some of these efforts in greater detail, but the focus of this colloquium is broader than the limited world of the College Board, and its agenda wider than that of 12 years ago. In 1970 the barriers to opportunity were perceived as educational and financial ones. Indeed, there was an assumption that we in education could float on favorable social and political tides to a landfall over and beyond the barriers of education and economics.

The trouble is that the tides have turned and have themselves become currents with which this conference, unlike the earlier one, must deal. Society's concern for its minorities, having waxed, now wanes. And its confidence in education, once strong, is weak. It is, as Michael Olivas writes, difficult to reconstruct the optimism in which the 1970 conference was conducted.

On the political scene, the electorate in 1970 was still, on balance, liberal in its leaning. In 1982 it is responsible for a conservative national administration. I am convinced that, in today's circumstances, the most serious barriers to educational opportunity are no longer the educational and financial ones but the social and political ones.

In 1970 Stephen Wright suggested that "the greatest of the barriers for minority/poverty youth is the barrier of money," and Humphrey Doerman concluded that "the most important financial aid issue of the day, and one critical to broadening the availability of college education, [was] whether or not significant amounts of new money [could] be made available to finance the obvious needs in ways that [would] meet those needs without producing severe and unwanted side effects."

I contend that we got a lot of the money we needed, but it generated both unwanted and unexpected side effects, including, but far from restricted to, the ones I have already cited. Both the public and the educational community got hooked on federal largesse (the unhooked federal purse, as Henry Halsted put it), as meeting need got translated into providing subsidy. Institutions began to lose their fiber, and the middle class was able to make money on loans supposedly taken out to pay for a college education. In the end the electorate decided that things had gone too far, and the current national administration is responding by demanding instant withdrawal from our addiction.

In the current climate, we in education must exert all the direct social and political pressure we can simply to restore the levels of support achieved earlier. This effort has to be a priority, now! The prognosis on this score, however, is not reassuring. Organizing for political action more effectively than ever before, the educational community nevertheless has yet to prove its viability as a political force. Preaching to politicians and the public and pleading for funds, by themselves, simply won't do the trick.

While we are preaching we will also have to act in ways that restore public confidence in education—to insure, for example, that money intended for student financial aid is not used for family financial subsidy, of course, but, even more important, to insure that money intended for all educational purposes brings a greater return in the form of educational product: fewer dropouts, higher levels of attainment, more demonstrable value added through learning for a much larger proportion of the population, for, as Ken Ashworth points out, "Society will likely support efforts to raise all groups to perform effectively against measures of achievement and competency."

And that is why I believe that greater and more lasting hope for effectively dealing with all of the barriers to higher education for minorities lies in quite another line of action—other, that is, than mere political mobilization. It is one that may seem to involve a paradox, because it requires raising one of the very barriers to educational opportunity that was identified here at Wingspread a dozen years ago. Proposing it may seem to place me at odds with many of you, but I believe the difference to be in appearance only, not in reality.

To be specific, I suggest that we use the new circumstance, the renewed national interest in the quality of education, to raise our expectations for entry to college—and thereby exert leverage on the quality of all of high school education—and at the same time devote our energies within education to finding the means, indeed demanding the means, to help minority youth meet those standards—those new, higher barriers, if you will.

Let me emphasize that I do not mean to help them artificially over the barrier by giving them bonus points on the SAT.

I have two reasons for this position.

First, we have already learned the hard way that getting over a barrier can be meaningless if you don't have the equipment to survive on the other side. For many—not for all, but for many—the "open door" to higher education did in fact turn out to be a revolving door. The very high rates of attrition, especially at "open door" institutions, despite large investments in remedial and compensatory programs, attest to its revolution.

Second, the mean scores, which display differences between minority students and the rest, mask a wide range of abilities among those who take the test—so wide that among the highest performers in a minority population are substantial numbers who equal or better most of the majority. (For example, on the verbal sections of the SAT in 1980, approximately 5,000 black students did better than 500,000 whites).

I am not taking a position against remedial and compensatory programs in the short run. I am not saying that students currently disadvantaged at the various points in the educational process will not need special help. I am saying that to eliminate barriers and provide educational opportunity to minority and disadvantaged youth, a far better way over the long run is to eliminate the need for such efforts by demanding and obtaining higher quality in education in the first place. But this cannot be done by mere exhortation. We must be willing to say what satisfactory quality is in concrete, doable terms. And the way to do that is in part through agreement on higher standards—higher standards not of selection but of enablement.

As Sandy Astin's report points out, inadequate preparation creates the educational barrier to higher education, and until we eliminate that inadequacy for all students, we will have to accept the continuation of some special treatment for those already disadvantaged. But do we really want to accept that palliative for an indefinite period? I think not, for what does such blanket stereotyping, however commendable the motives, do for those in such a group who need no compensatory treatment or, indeed, for the group itself when there are other means available to achieve the same goals?

I believe that the "E" element in our Educational EQuality Project is one such alternative. We say that the E in the capital EQ stands for Equality, and the Q for Quality. But we say more: we say that the E also stands for Enablement in quality and to meet standards. Therefore I suggest to you that a new call for higher standards of educational quality is or should be an inherent part of any effective attack on the barriers to educational opportunity—and one that uses the leverage of a not entirely friendly political and social climate in behalf of opportunity rather than fights against it.

In summary, the nature of the barriers to higher education has changed since the last colloquium that dealt with these things here at Wingspread a dozen years ago. Political and social barriers have arisen in part as unexpected consequences of the changes we sought to bring about. The economic barrier to higher education has been lowered, as we declared it needed to be, but it now promises to rise again in tandem with, and as a function of, the new social and political barriers.

These new circumstances call for differential treatment of today's barriers. On the one hand, we need an immediate frontal attack on the political and social barriers in order to tear them down. On the other, one strategy within education must not be to lower, let alone destroy, the former barriers, but to eliminate the conditions that make them barriers—the "prior barriers" if you will, of inadequate preparation and inadequate standards of quality and enablement in the schools. This requires multiple strategies and many participants, but I believe one essential element is to reaffirm and raise our expectations of what the schools will do to prepare students for higher education—to support standards, not as a code for discrimination, but as a demand for inclusion, and to create, somehow, that alliance that Ed Gordon calls for between those who would conserve opportunity and those of us who would expand it.

Yes, we need to find ways to help students to get over the barriers, but in ways that do not leave them on the other side unable to cope with the demands of the new environment of higher education.

That is how, ultimately, we will help minority students to more and better educational opportunity—by improving our product in ways that will not just satisfy the national search for quality in education, but also prepare more minority students to meet a higher standard of entry to higher education.

Editor's note:

George Hanford was not left unchallenged. One questioner asked whether minority youth were not being shunted into "trivial" occupations; he agreed that this was a potential problem and urged the postsecondary community to reach earlier into students' careers, for instance through work with high schools. Another participant wondered whether Hanford's educational strategies could solve what were essentially political problems—as in the situ-

ation of some inner-city schools that, with the best motives, are prevented from being effective because they are provided with comparatively few resources. The speaker contended that there is still cause for hope, giving as an example a situation in which two schools identical in student body, locale, and resources produce very different results.

The most somber note was struck by a number of speakers who pointed out that, for minority populations, "raising standards" has typically been a code word for exclusionary practices, and that "qualified" has more often than not meant "white." They urged the group not to ignore the real gains of the last decade while concentrating on the new emphasis on quality. There was general agreement that careful attention to the quality issue must be a major theme of the conference.

The Social and Ethical Context of Special Programs

Edmund W. Gordon

The efforts of the past 20 years to equalize more extensively opportunities for blacks and other ethnic minorities in higher education can be viewed as a continuation of the long history of democratization of educational opportunity in human societies. Over the past several centuries we have seen basic and advanced or higher education become available to ever wider segments of most populations. Once the unique priviledge of the nobility (religious and political), the opportunity to become educated slowly was expanded so as to permit access as a result of meritocratic as well as aristocratic status. Whether merit was to be judged by traditional indexes of developed academic ability, athletic prowess, family position (all of which have been influential in Western European and American higher education), or political affiliation (as is reported to have been influential in China and some other socialist countries), or previously bypassed target group membership (which has received some emphasis in socialist and capitalist approaches to affirmative action), all these efforts are based on some inferred entitlement as a basis for selection. However, only developed academic ability and family position have consistently dominated access to education in general and higher education in particular, while athletic prowess continues to provide some degree of advantage. As the difficulties which seem to adhere to teaching nontraditional populations through higher education have become more obvious and the consequences of failure more apparent, the Socialist countries have given less emphasis to political affiliation and both capitalist and socialist countries have reduced the attention given to previously bypassed target group status as bases for special consideration in access to higher education.

Not only the difficulties involved in teaching nontraditional poulations have led to this declining emphasis. Rather the capital investments perceived to be required for economic and military survival in the modern world are such that together with a worldwide depression in economic growth, national policy in the nations of the world has not favored greater investment in human capital development. In fact, we see an interesting paradox reflected in our awareness that greater dependence on technology requires greater technological literarcy and better education at the same time that our faith in the functional utility of advanced educational development is in decline. The only rational basis for this apparent contradiction is to be found in the assumption that advanced technological societies will require high-level intellectual and educational development of only a small minority of our populations, while the intellect and competence of the majority will be superfluous and therefore unneeded and justifiably neglected. Such a rationale is both socially destructive and ethically repugnant. It is to issues related to these social and ethical (moral) contexts that this paper is directed.

Special programs of service to populations not traditionally served by higher education are new and old. Twelve years ago, when I spoke here at a previous conference on higher education and the disadvantaged, I was remined, following what was, I thought, brilliant review of earlier versions of special programs, that the traditionally black colleges have been serving such populations for a much longer time than had the colleges and universities I included in my mid-1960s study. These predominantly black institutions historically have responded to the tragic social reality of racism which has been manifested in so much of the history of education in the United States. We would be remiss should we fail to acknowledge that differential and prejudicial treatment based on ethicity, sex, and social class is a ubiquitous element in the social context in which special programs were born, reinvented, and continue to be maintained. Although we have made relatively substantial progress in reducing bias based on all three of these characteristics, it is bias based on ethnic caste status which appears to be most recalcitrant. Even in the presence of real efforts at the elimination of the negative effects of such bias, the intergenerational effects of opportunity denial confront us with developmental challenges that defy easy solution. Yet any efforts at special services must be concerned with the implications of racism in its institutional, individual, and group oppressor manifestations.

Special programs of service to populations not traditionally served by higher education, like the populations to which they are directed, have been denied opportunity. They have been denied an adequate opportunity to succeed by virtue of their having been undercapitalized conceptually and financially. There are few if any theories of late adolescent and young adult underdevelopment or of the developmental learning needs of lower caste populations which can be used to inform our special programs. There is little systematic knowledge concerning the learning behavior of ethnic minority populations whose relationship to the dominant cultural and ethnic groups is traditionally defined as marginal. The conceptual capital that has been invested in special programs has been borrowed from postulates referrable to remediation and compensation (an error for which I must assume a portion of the responsibility) or at best from the patronizing perspective of preparations for the failure to respond adequately to the facts of cultural difference when the establishment was preoccupied with concern for alleged "cultural deprivation." Programs that were lacking in good ideas could hardly have used well the monetary resources made available to them. When we add the fact that few of these programs were adequately and consistently well funded, one does not need to be labor the fact that they have a long history of fiscal undercapitalization.

The social context of special programs includes the paradox of contradiction with which their host institutions struggle as a reflection of the contradictions in the society that has given birth to them. Mao Tse Tung has written a beautiful essay on contradiction. He reminds us that it is a feature of all phenomena; everything has its opposites, and, to complicate things even more, these contradictions are in dynamic states—that is, they are in a consistent and constant state of change. When one aspect of the contradiction is in the ascendancy, the opposite is in the descendancy; the fact that aspect A of the contradiction is ascending today does not mean that it will always be in the ascending position—it may reverse itself. The trick, of course, is to recognize the actual position of these polar extremes at a given point in time and to adjust one's behavior or one's program in relation to them.

Jean-Paul Sartre has also struggled with the paradox of contradiction and fortunatley has recognized its impact on the role and function of the intellectual as well as on the role and function of those institutions charged with the responsibility for the nurturnace of intellect, such as the university. Intellectuals and universities in their roles as nurturers of intellect are caught in a paradox of contradiction because they are, by their very nature, conservationist or conservative—conservative of the traditions, the collective experience, the acquired knowledge of man. Pardoxically, however, one who has acquired intellect has in the process become committed to criticism, which can only give birth to change. Intellect and intellect-producing institutions then are, at one and the same time, conservative and revolutionary. The intellectual and the universities tend to be liberal; in our society they have traditionally been the advocates of democracy; because of heightened understanding and sensitivity they are more likely to be humanitarian; still, we have yet to discover a way of nurturing and rewarding intellect that is not elitist or at least meritocratic rather than democratic. The university is a society-serving institution; however, in order to achieve this purpose, which includes the nurturance of the society's intellect, it seems to have to be insulated from the society it serves. It stimulates change and diversity, but it nurtures conformity. It is ideally committed to the development of intellect but functionally committed to producing credentials and skills. What my friend and mentor W. E. B. DuBois called "the liberating arts and sciences" have come to be thought of as rather useless, while vocational, technical, and professional programs have flourished.

This contradiction between the idealized commitment and the functional development of the university has been discussed in another context by Anthony Wallace, the anthropologist. He talks about education and its roles and functions in societies in different phases of their development; it may be that Wallace's treatment of the contradiction most clearly points to the relevance of contradiction in education of the poor. Wallace talks about morality, intellect, and skills as essential purposes of education and the dialectical or dynamic relationship of these three purposes as societies move from their revolutionary phase to a conservative phase to a reactionary phase. He suggests that in the conservative society first attention is given to skill development because the development of skills is essential to the maintenance of that society. He argues that the next level of attention is given to moral development, which I see as socialization, how one gets along in a society; and only third-level attention is given to the development of intellect. By the time society reaches its reactionary phase, moral development has become law and order: "What does the State expect of me?" Second-level attention is given to skill development (techniques): "How do I serve the society?", and little or no attention is given to intellect. Wallace wrote that essay in 1960, but it is interesting to see how appropriate it is to the late 1960s and the early 1970s, when the university came under attack and when the greatest attention in our society with regard to education was given to career education or vocational education. Our expectation of our public schools, of our universities, and of our colleges was to teach people how to enter the labor force and how to become productive persons. Wallace reminds us that in none of these phases of societale development is primary attention given to the development of intellect; intellect tends to be neglected in all of them, or at least it tends not to have priority in any of them.

A point Wallace does not make is that the various elements of society move through these phases at different rates, so that while the dominant interest of the ruling group in society may be conservative or reactionary, as we can see in this country over the recent period, there are elements in the society that may be in a revolutionary phase. If we look at the young people whom we are concerned with—at poor people, at ethnic minorities, at low-status people—we find that they are, or should be, very much concerned with change, with radical change and revolution, rather that conservatism and reaction. We are in a position in which the university puts conservatism and reaction in the ascendency and revolution in a descending position, while the young people we are trying to introduce into the system that the university represents have a different set of values— revolutionary values. This conflict becomes a force that is a drag on successful upward movement of these young people. Thus when the university reaches out to democratize but uses elitist models in the service of a reactionary society, the contradictions are so obvious that it should come as no surprise that we fail as often as we succeed.

The status of our program is also conditional, because it its conservative or reactionary phase the nation is turning from expanding opportunity to conserving opportunity, from a democratic back to a meritocratic—and maybe even an aristocratic—basis for the selection and support of students. Here I refer to the steadily rising cost of higher education coupled with the erosion of opportunity for the poor as a function of the conservation of opportunity for the middle-income group. My interest is not to put one group against the other, but if we are going to increase the pool of eligible candidates to include lower-income groups, as I think we should, we must also increase the pool of resources to accommodate the added numbers and the increased costs. If we are to protect our programs and reduce their conditional state, it may be necessary to form an alliance between those who would conserve opportunity and those of us who would expand opportunity.

Given the essentially destructive social context in which special programs function and the ethically repugnant character of the current climate in which these programs must exist, where do we turn for guidance? What conceptual frames can possibly inform policy on postsecondary programs for the disadvantaged? In his provocative work *A Theory of Justice*,[1] John Rawls has advanced two principles of justice and two priority rules, leading to a general conception that should have utility for our work. The following summarizes Rawls's idea.

First Principle:
> Each person is to have an equal right to the most extensive total system of equal basic liberties compatible with a similar system of liberty for all.

---

1. John Rawls, *A Theory of Justice*. Cambridge, Massachusetts: Bellknap Press, 1971, pages 302-3.

Second Principle:
Social and economic inequalities are to be arranged so that they are both:
a. to the greatest benefit of the least advantaged, consistent with the just savings principle, and
b. attached to offices and positions open to all under conditions of fair equality of opportunity.
First Priority Rule (The Priorty of Liberty):
The principles of justice are to ranked in lexical order and therefore liberty can be restricted only for the sake of liberty. There are two cases:
a. a less extensive liberty must strengthen the total system of liberty shared by all;
b. a less than equal liberty must be acceptable to those with the lesser liberty.
Second Priority Rule (The Priority of Justice over Efficiency and Welfare):
The second principle of justice is lexically prior to the principle of efficiency and to that of maximizing the sum of advantages; and fair opportunity is prior to the difference principle. There are two cases:
a. an inequality of opportunity must enhance the opportunities of those with lesser opportunity;
b. an excessive rate of saving must on balance mitigate the burden of those bearing this hardship.
General Conception:
All social primary goods—liberty and opportunity, income and wealth, and the bases of self-respect—are to be distributed equally unless an unequal distribution of any or all of these goods is to the advantage of the least favored.

The ethnical and moral basis for special programs resides in a philosophical commitment to social justice, which our society has yet to make real. Aside from such impediments to social justice as racism, economic exploitation, ursurpation of power, and the perpetuation of ignorance, it may well be that our society has never accepted tor understood the full implications of this noble ideal. We are indebted to Rawls for drawing the issues more clearly. Even if we were to accept his notion of priority concern for the least advantaged, our tradition of defining such groups by their *status* misleads us and hopelessly truncates our search for solutions. As important as are the disadvantages that are imposed on groups that are defined by their lower-class position, or ethnic and gender caste positions, it may well be that it is the differences in the functional characteristics of learners that make for the most significant obstacles in learning and educational development. One's status primarily influences how one is perceived, the nature of opportunities provided, the kind and amount of resources, the role to which one is likely to be assigned.

All these can be major sources of advantage or disadvantage. However, the way in which one functions—for example, one's affective and cognitive response tendencies, one's sources of identity and motivation, etc.—determines the manner in which one responds to the way one is perceived, to the opportunity made available, and to the resources and roles that are available. Yet it is the functional characteristics that have largely been ignored. Educational programs, court decisions, legislation, affirmative action programs—all have been influenced by the status characteristics of the people, but for purposes of education these status characteristics do not define educational need or inform pedagogical intervention. The least favored or those with lesser liberty, to use Rawls's terms, may well be those whose functional characteristics are not complemented by standard educational treatments, those whom our institutional forms have never been designed to serve. Rawls's conception of justice requires that all status groups be treated equally except that any inequalities must be to the greatest benefit of the least advantaged. When we include both status and functional characteristics as our basis for determining disadvantagement, we are forced to look beyond a concern for one's equal share to one's essential needs. If we are to provide the greatest benefit to the least advantaged, the criterion must be sufficiency, not equality.

This conception has implications for what we do in special services.

1. The target groups for our services must be defined by their functional characteristics as well as their status.

2. Adequate programs of service must be based on sophisticated diagnostic facilities, since functional needs cannot be inferred accurately from status data.

3. Appropriate conceptual models, adequate financial and material resources, and competent human resources must be made available.

4. It may be necesary that our best institutional and human resources be made available in order that social and economic inequities be arranged so that they are to the greatest benefit of the least advantaged.

My colleagues who follow will be talking about a variety of criteria and models for good special services programs, but none is likely to meet the standard advanced by the late Hugh Lane in his University of Utopia.[2] I am pleased to share his brilliant conception with you.

Toward Utopia, by Hugh Lane

. . . The University of Utopia [is] a far place clearly seen, a vision of full societal participation in the purposes and benefits of education.

I have been privileged from time to time to visit the nation of Utopia and to

---

2. The following quotation is taken from an article that appeared originally in the *IRCD Bulletin* of the Information Retrieval Center on the Disadvantaged, New York, Teachers College of Columbia University, 1970.

observe its University and to discuss the theory and practice of the higher learning with members of its faculty and student body. Many of the issues which consume our time and energy seem not to exist there possibly because education is conceived by Utopians as central to the continuity of their social and political processes and therefore it has the highest priority in planning and expenditure of public funds.

Every citizen, every human being is expected to be involved in the universal education system at the level appropriate to his stage of development. This seems to mean that the University of Utopia has an open admissions policy. It was necessary at one stage of their history to make it a matter of public policy that expenditure for education came first in order that there be a place in the education system for each person born into the nation.

Each level of education in Utopia has a charter covering a delimited area of content and skill, and each educational institution is licensed to offer degree programs and to administer certification procedures within its level or levels.

Interestingly enough, psychometrics is the key to educational planning and practice in Utopia. Tests and measurements are the primary tool for guidance and placement, and the concept of admissions as we use it has disappeared. Each student regularly participates in a national assessment which rates him relative to the achievement of the goals in a core curriculum composed of basic life skills and citizen responsibilities.

Persons rated as having attained the level of mastery in the collegiate skills and responsibilities are awarded the appropriate degree regardless of the mode of preparation or their age or sex or any other extraneous criterion. There are thus any number of esteemed scholars who never participated in the formal educational system while others spent varying lengths of time as required in the individual case to master the skills and behaviors represented in the core curriculum.

The rule of thumb for placement of those entering college work involves dividing the student population into thirds. Those rated in the upper third along any parameter of skill or behavior are not allowed to participate in formal instruction in preparing themselves for terminal comprehensive examination. The total resources of the University are available to them for independent study and independent study is what is exacted. The Utopian experience is that every student prepares some area independently while it is not unusual for some students to satisfy the entire collegiate requirement in this manner.

Students in the middle third are organized into advisory groupings with preceptors and advisors assigned to guide them in their preparation for examination. In some areas instruction is available for this group, though the student is moved toward independent study as rapidly as his development warrants.

The lower end of the entering student body begins its collegiate education in formally organized courses of study. The best teachers in the system are available to conduct these courses. Interestingly enough, the highest awards in terms of salary and prerogative are bestowed on these members of the Utopian faculty. Students from the upper and middle thirds are often hired under a work-study arrangement as tutors, teaching assistants and study partners for this group. Thus instruction and learning is not confined to the classroom, but is extended to the living sector, the recreational sector, and the laboratory. Students in this lower third can often earn extra money stipends for working closely with the research faculty under fairly close guidance and supervision. Most replications of basic research are carried out in this manner.

With education defined as preparation for comprehensive examination, it came as something of a shock to me to discover that the examinations are published. In this way every candidate for an examination knows roughly what he will face under comprehensive examination. This may explain the relatively large proportion of the population which achieves degree status without formal instruction. This whole area bothered me, but the administration seemed unbothered by it, since the institutions are not economically dependent upon student fees for time served. Many students noted that the systematic study of previous examinations was in actuality a concrete way of apprehending the objectives of the course area under study.

The development of this multi-modal, many-tracked approach to the higher learning is attributed by many to Benjamin Bloom, who evidently reinterpreted John Carroll's hypotheses on testing and learning to show that for practical purposes all students can be brought to the level of mastery given proper manipulation of the dimensions of time, method and medium of instruction. Bloom's paper, entitled "Learning for Mastery,"[3] is revered almost as much as the Utopian Bible.

I could not find at the University of Utopia any counterpart for the financial aid officer. In discussion with their administrators I tried to raise the question of the responsibility of the parent to contribute directly to the economic support of the child in college. Utopian educators found this idea laughable and characterized it as counter-educational. "How, indeed," they asked, "can one inculcate independence of mind while enforcing economic dependence upon one's forebears?" The ruthlessness of their logic eventually blew my mind—for I saw exactly how they had made education the promise of the total society rather than the prerogative of the economically better endowed. Each student, and this includes all persons, is paid a living wage in Utopia. Each learns that he has the possibility of producing alteration of his life style and position and that he is neither propelled nor unduly hampered by the personal accident of birth. Since any individual may truly become the President of Utopia, it is seen as urgent that all individuals be prepared for ultimate responsibility.

The Utopians not only demolished the idea of parents' contribution for me; they destroyed the notion of tuition. So clearly had the society opted to provide the total cost of total education for all its citizens that the notion of additional cost to be recovered was foreign. When I described our own practices, they characterized tuition–parental contribution as a version of the means test, long outlawed in Utopian society. Much of their reasoning seems to be rooted in the

---

3. Benjamin S. Bloom. "Learning for Mastery," *Evaluation Comment*, Vol. 1, No. 2. May, 1968 (Los Angeles: Center for the Study of Evaluation of Instructional Programs, U.C.L.A.).

idea of full individual participation in the governance of the nation. If each man has one vote, it behooves the society to be certain that each vote is an informed one and leaving this to the vagaries of economic level of birth would seem ludicrous to any Utopian.

I looked long and hard for the counterpart of our chattel slave-athlete. What I actually found was a group of students specializing in Physical Recreation, its principles and practice. Spectator sports as we know them were not present at the University of Utopia. Athletics was so broadly based that there were seldom enough spectators to support an industrial approach to athletics. Participatory sports was the vogue. Every student was on some kind of team or engaged in individual exercise. The Utopians seem to believe that a healthy mind exists in a healthy active body—when that is necessary in the individual case.

Colleges, by the way, were not the only post-secondary experience I noted in Utopia. That is, not all Utopians worked toward formal certification via the degree route. Apprenticeship and on-the-job training were acceptable and in many cases the preferred route to economic maturity. As the Utopians believed in a policy of full employment, they disavowed artificial or irrelevant criteria for hiring or employment.

I don't fully understand how the Utopians have developed this system without rearing a cumbersome unwieldly bureaucracy, but it is interesting to note that the "ombudsman" role is formalized and highly developed. The "Office of Renewal" is devoted to the continual study of Utopian institutional forms and procedures. Continuity is valued by those in this office but their greatest delight is in the devising of streamlined efficient procedures. The best minds in the society are available for work in this Office and every societal form and procedure is subjected to periodic review and revision.

It might be important to note that this office is situated at the national level and funded centrally and also that it has no permanent personnel. All persons in the society are expected to contemplate its institutional forms and to influence them. It would never occur to a Utopian to leave so essential an area to the experts, so as an alternative all Utopians have developed this particular expertise.

These observations of practices in Utopia are offered not as definitive of desired practice for you in our nation at this time in our history. Rather they are palpable evidence that *our* practices are not the only way it can be done, they are not necessarily the best way we could do it. Let us subject our present practices to ruthless analysis, giving them up if necessary to achieve some better, more harmonious educational goal in which the maximal development of each student committed to our charge is seen as our highest goal and no person born into our society is excluded from the body of students of which we treat.

Need for Continous Reevaluation

In the decade ahead we Americans will dissect the implications of open admissions to higher education. The lessons from Utopia would suggest that our entire life style is up for review. We must rethink the arrangements of our institutions of higher learning into public/private, well-endowed/poor. We must examine the socio-political implications of the financing of higher education, questioning whether parental contribution to the education of the child is consistent with the theory of democratic participation by an educated electorate. Clearly we must reevaluate the potential of psychometrics and educational testing, devising ways maximally to develop individual potential for service to the society while providing both safeguards for individual privacy and avoiding the rearing of another cumbersome, impossible bureaucracy unamendable to orderly change and development.

In the intervening period and till this Utopian perspective is achieved, we at National Scholarship Service and Fund for Negro Students and Aspira and in the Talent Search field must continue to pursue our special advocacy of the Black, the Chicano, the Indian, the Appalachian, the southern poor white, and the Puerto Rican in order to achieve our share of America. We do this not from separatism but in order to make the promise of this experimetn in democracy real.

If we approach these tasks which face us now in 1970, the nineteen eighties may see the achievement of a Utopian perspective in our time and on our scene.

We know that the attainment of this perspective depends not upon you alone. Those who govern us must realize that expenditure for the development of human potential cannot be called inflationary. The taxpayer must become a true revolutionary and demand a return in the form of first things first. The students, our hope for Utopia, must persevere in protest and in learning. Our faculties must encounter the learner where he is and not just where they are. The new perspective will be attained for it must be attained. . . .

Response by Frederick S. Humphries

Admittedly, our nation is engaged today in the undoing of the Great Society program. Conservatism and supply-side economic thought serve to undermine the nation's perspective, its social programs, and its economic policy development. There is a prevalent obsession with increasing the military might of our armed forces, presumably to achieve "first" status among military powers. At the same time, it has become clear that America cannot support, alone, the military defense of the free world and also treat its own internal social and economic problems. As I studied Edmund Gordon's paper, "The Social and Ethical Context of Special Programs," I found much with which I can agree. There are also points on which I would like to comment.

In an essay on the aims of general education, "A Quest for Common Learning," Ernest L. Boyer and Arthur Levine noted the rising chorus of complaints about the quality of schooling and the importance of more public support for education for the well-being of our society. They believe that the quality-of-schooling discussion has ushered in a period that has witnessed a "national rush to reduce investments in education," to 'shift resources disproportionately away from education, and to forsake the public schools—where 90 percent of our children are now enrolled."

One of their themes in this provocative essay is that the racial and ethnic composition of the public school system is changing at a time when the number of students depending more heavily on public education is on the increase. Since 1970 the proportions of Hispanics and blacks in the public school system have increased in New York, Miami, and in 20 of the largest urban districts of the United States. As the percentage of black and Hispanic students increases, there is a decrease in the number of whites attending public schools, and thus "white America's commitment to education may well decline."

During much of the century, Boyer and Levine contend, the American system worked reasonably well for those students who attended. A high school education was considered adequate for all but a small number of professional pursuits. The shifting base of the economy has changed all of this as old jobs disappear and new ones emerge. If this society wants "higher intellectual and economic productivity, a larger stock of both non-human and human capital will be needed." To support the need for more education beyond the traditional 12 years of formal education, they note the accelerating trend toward specialization and the increase in the number of professionals and technical workers in the work force.

To support their thesis that technological advances require more widespread literacy there is no better example than the military, in which "equipment has already become more sophisticated than the available labor force and where buying more hardware seems unwise unless accompanied by at least a comparable investment in the people who will have to use it." Thus "the work place is changing drastically," traditional notions about pre-work preparation are becoming obsolete and "more education will be required to meet the nation's diverse social and economic needs."

They conclude with the observation that failure adequately to educate at public expense a new generation of students "would be a shocking denial of their rights and a fatal undermining of the vital interests of the nation. . . . Our efforts must be redoubled to meet more effectively the needs of those who have been inadequately serve by education in the past."

Gordon believes that the nation is turning from expanding opportunity to conserving opportunity in the selection and support of its students. As evidence of this conservative movement in higher education he cites three areas that are especially significant: (1) the rising cost of education, (2) the erosion of opportunity for the poor, and (3) tuition tax credits, which he sees as a mechanism to expand opportunity for middle-income over lower-income groups.

With the recent cuts in education programs on the federal level, some believe that these lost funds will be replaced by state governments. But statistics indicate that states are having problems, too, as tuition costs have increased at a rapid rate and state budgets are tightened in all areas. The National Association of American Universities and the National Association of State Universities and Land-Grant Colleges (NASULGC) reported that their institutions' fees rose 17.7 percent in 1981–82 from the previous year, and that "total education costs are over $4,000 per year at many of its institutions." At least 31 states have cut higher education funding, ranging from 24 pecent in Washington to 10 pecent in Utah and Pennsylvania.

Another myth is that the erosion of opportunity will not occur under the current administration's proposed cuts. But, according to President Robert L. Clodius of NASULGC, the facts do not support this conclusion. Indeed, the reduction of federal support will have a tremendous impact on low-income students in general and black educational institutions in particular.

The Pell Grant maximum award, which goes to the neediest students, would be cut almost 12 percent from $1,800 to $1,600, bringing it down to the level of fiscal year 1978. A student from a family of four earning $12,000, living on campus at a four-year institution would have the award cut from $1,400 to $810.

The elimination of the Supplemental Educational Opportunity Grant program would seriously hurt low-income students. According to the Department of Education's *Student Aid Handbook* of July 1981, only 2.6 percent of SEOG recipients in academic year 1978–79 (the most recent year for which data are available) were from families with incomes above $25,000, while only 12.2 percent were about $18,000. Several hundred thousand low-income students will be deprived of their awards.

The administration's argument that a low-income student can receive $9,100 in aid is deceptive and misleading. A student would have to be simultaneously poor enough to receive a maximum Pell award of $1,600 (less than $10,000 income for a family of four) and wealthy enough to pay back loans of $7,500 a year. Three thousand dollars of this would be a parent loan, which requires the parent to repay at 14 percent interest starting 60 days after disbursement. This student and his family would be $30,000 in debt plus interest on graduation. The hypothetical student would have to have one parent on welfare and the other employed as a bank president to handle this situation!

The administration says students who lose Pell Grants can get GSLs instead, but, according to the department's *Annual Evaluation Report* for fiscal 1980, 48 percent of students who received GSLs were already receiving Pell Grants.

As president of a historically black college, I am aware of the impact these cuts will have on these institutions. Over time, black colleges have had very large percentages of their student body on some form of federal aid, since the students' families are predominantly low income. As mentioned earlier, Pell awards for the neediest students are proposed for a 12 percent cut, and the SEOG program, which serves mainly low-income students, will be eliminated. Data from the Department of Education itself point out that minority students (black, Asian, Hispanic, and American Indian) comprised 56.7 percent of Pell recipients in 1978–79 but comprised only 22.5 percent of undergraduate enrollment.

There is no question that minority students and black colleges will be devastated by the effects of the combined cuts in Pell, SEOG, National Direct Student Loans and other programs. In addition, the severe reduction proposed for TRIO support services will make it more difficult for minorities to enroll and graduate.

Gordon's observation that "if we are going to increase the pool of eligible candidates to include lower-income groups and thus democratize education—we must also increase the pool of resources to accommodate the added numbers and the increased cost" best summarizes the contradictions in higher education as it relates to the disadvantaged.

John Rawls's *A Theory of Justice* as a conceptual framework to "inform policy on post-secondary programs for the disadvantaged" is a concept I can support. The notion advanced that each person has a right to the most extensive basic liberties compatible with a similar system of liberty for all is one that I believe in. I also can support the idea that social and economic inequalities should be arranged so that they are to the greater benefit of the least advantaged and that offices and positions should be opened to all under conditions of fair equality of opportunity.

However, the general conception that "all social and primary goods— liberty and opportunity, income and wealth, and the bases of self-respect are to be distributed equally unless an unequal distribution of any of these goods is to the advantage of the least favored" is a theory that is not practical in undergirding special programs, for a number of reasons. The primary reason is that the mind set of the policy makers who initiate and develop special programs is different. Even if decision makers and policy makers recognized the need for "compensated" justice to be achieved by giving more to those who have been discriminated against as a way of compensation, the idea is so revolutionary in its context that it would not be acceptable. Thus practically justice cannot be obtained.

Gordon is of the opinion that special programs have been denied an adequate opportunity to succeed because they have been "undercapitalized conceptually and financially." He deplores the notion that "there are few if any theories of late adolescent and young adult underdevelopment or of the developmental learning needs of lower caste populations which can be used to inform our special programs." I would agree that both statements are true. Special programs have been poorly conceptualized and in many instances underfinanced. Perhaps there is no well-documented body of knowledge that is a sure-fire cure to advance the cognitive and affective skills of the disadvantaged with the advantaged students of our society. But part of the reason for this is not in the conceptualization of special programs, but in the way that society responds to problems.

The decision-making process affecting the solving of our nation's social problems is elitist. The great propensity in our society is for selecting people to seek solutions for social problems not because they are involved in the problem, but because they hold positions in elitist institutions and situations and are consequently distant from the problem. The Northeast Corridor, for example, gave inspiration to the Great Society programs. The choice of this group to conceptualize and formulate many of the programs in the Great Society and the fact that the nation paid attention to it was basically an elitist decision. The supposition was that the planners and organizers, by virtue of the fact that they worked at esteemed citadels of higher education, had the greater insight into how to solve the social and economic problems of our day. The decision makers and policy makers thus gave credence to their theories and notions.

On the other hand, those people who were working in the least-advantaged environment, who were familiar with the problems, and who had ideas of how to develop programs to address them were not thought to be legitimate enough to develop national policy. In the minds of the policy makers their experiences with the problems were discounted.

There are also a number of special programs that have been developed and conducted according to systematic notions about how to work effectively with ethnic minority populations described as having marginal skills. These programs have been based on self-concept and committed to the use of instructional materials related to the environmental and cultural aspect of the least-advantaged groups. They have been tremendously successful at the higher education level but have not found their way into the established body of knowledge nor captured the imagination of the nation. The reason for this is that the architects of such programs have not been the traditional architects. They were generally people from the least-advantaged sector and thus could not get the support of society at large. One such program was the Thirteen College Curriculum program. The conceptualization, method, and everything connected with the program came from people who were associated with the historically black colleges and universities. It was highly successful, yet given to ignominy in 1982.

Indeed, as noted in Gordon's paper, one of the major exceptions to the ambivalence about special programs has always been the success of the historically black colleges. These institutions over their lifetime have been devoted to and have carried out "special programs" that have rectified the neglect arising out of the racial, sex, and class distinctions in our society. They have been the one example in the context of this paper that is successful and on target in shifting people from least-advantaged to advantaged positions in our society.

This has been especially true of the relationship between these colleges and black people. Today the success of their educational programs and their ability to produce change in the social status of blacks are deeply threatened. In states where these colleges are located the obsession with "quality" is driving many of them toward meritocratic and aristocratic admissions policies. Institutions that were once open admissions institutions are now developing or have developed admissions requirements that will deny higher education to many who are disadvantaged. When this process is complete, it is clear that a large number of students who are now admitted will not be admitted later on.

For me, Gordon's paper was an enjoyable interlude. However, I don't expect it to serve as an instrument for any meaningful set of actions related to the forward movement of our society or as an underpinning of an attack on class, sex, or racial discrimination in higher education.

Editor's note:

The subsequent discussion with Ed Gordon focused on two questions: how to match better the range of educational "treatments" our institutions have to offer with the diversity of students (with emphasis on getting past such stereotypes as gender or ethnicity to individuals' learning characteristics), and how to move proven techniques from the purview of the special programs—which have indeed incorporated some of the approach discussed in the first question—to general college practices.

This observer had the impression that much of Gordon's presentation would have to be absorbed by the group over a long period of time, but that he had set out an ethical grounding that would be reflected in all subsequent discussions.

The Role of Government and the Private Sector

James M. Rosser

Let me begin by making a statement that is specifically exaggerated and intended to startle and establish some disequilibrium: I, for one, am glad that we will be faced with a reduced federal role in higher education. Let me compound the felony by adding that I am *particularly* glad that post-secondary programs for the educationally disadvantaged will be affected by this reduction in resources.

If we can accept the premise that the existential disequilibrium that has made this conference necessary will be sustained even beyond the time we spend here, then perhaps we can understand the thrust of my initial remarks, which are intended also to remind us that significant change most often involves a period of disequilibrium, upset, and disintegration out of which a new equilibrium is established.

Most of the conversations I hear on this issue betray a faint but unmistakable hint of addictive dependency. Addictive dependency suggests that if we don't get our separate "fix" of tax dollars, everything that we have accomplished over the past 20 years will dry up and blow away. It suggests that work that has engaged many of us for just about all of our professional lives will somehow, overnight, become meaningless.

Part of the fear of future withdrawal of tax dollars comes from the suspicion (which in some institutions and in some state programs borders on absolute certainty) that we won't be able to convince elected officials, institutional leaders, or taxpayers that what we are doing is worthy of continued support. Put more crudely, many of us fear that our Educational Opportunity Programs (EOP) wouldn't stand up to the kind of rigorous scrutiny that would prove unequivocally that they have really made a difference—a scrutiny that now is routinely applied to other types of educational programs competing for scarce dollars.

Think about this for a minute. How many of us run programs whose lifeblood depends on tax dollars and/or the largesse of a college's trustees? How long would it take any of us to mount a convincing argument that our state or our institution would suffer "a significant loss" were such programs to fold up and go away? I maintain that if it requires a Ph.D. in statistics to understand the argument, then our fears are justified.

I would also suggest that the plight many of us believe ourselves to be in is not the fault of Ronald Reagan, the Republican Party, or even John Q. Public, the average American taxpayer. The fault is, unfortunately, primarily our own. It is our own because we failed to do some very crucial planning for this era of scarcity (which we all told each other was coming), which is now here and which we are—as this conference so convincingly demonstrates—poorly prepared to confront.

The first of our failures was that when we developed a quality product we failed miserably to replicate it. I know, for example, from my tenure as the Vice Chancellor of Higher Education in New Jersey, that that state's higher education program for the disadvantaged had a number of excellent programs that boasted of high student achievement and low annual attrition. These programs attracted motivated students who not only earned high academic honors but also, by their presence, enriched the campuses they had chosen to attend. Alas, these programs were all too rare.

There were also, however, large numbers of institutions in which just the opposite was in evidence. These programs reported annual attrition rates as high as 75 percent or greater per year. Academically, the majority of the students struggled to attain minimal performance standards. In all too many instances, apologists for these programs argued, and successfully I might add, that the best solution to the problem of subpar performance was remediation, a posture that quietly resulted in the lowering of expectations and standards. Thus, longer probation periods were created, lower performance standards were adopted, and more aid was provided—essentially to help students achieve *less* and at a slower rate!

Is it any wonder, therefore, that many of us are afraid that the taxpayer won't foot the bill any longer? Is it any wonder that a college official can be quoted in the Astin study as saying, in effect, that educating minority students is passé? Why shouldn't he believe this? After all, the programs were separately funded—i.e., not integrated into institutional base budgets—and if producing an inferior product failed to stop the flow of dollars, why should any college feel a responsibility to change its practices? No one disputed the claim that disadvantaged students required special aid to complete college. The real "beef," if you will, was that we appeared to be asking for a handout, on the one hand, but were arguing that our folk shouldn't have to work as hard or do as much for it, on the other.

What did it matter, therefore, that some programs consistently achieved high standards? The simple fact that the results-oriented programs were in the minority has meant that there has not been nor will there be a widespread public outcry over the loss of our federal and/or state fix, when and if it happens. For some programs such an outcry will be heard, but these, I maintain, will be the exception, not the rule.

Which brings me to the next in my list of our failures—namely, the lack of a "spillover effect." A spillover effect would have been produced if all students—not just blacks, or Chicanos, or Native Americans—had benefited from the existence of our efforts. Evidence of a spillover effect would entail, for example, having nonminority students with academic skills deficiencies benefit as much as minority students from exposure to the best of the techniques and practices that the most successful EO programs had to offer. This presumes, of course, the existence of diagnostic and prescriptive services in these programs—services that have been articulated with institutional curriculum standards and achievement expectations.

I do not say that many nondisadvantaged students failed to benefit from the existence of these programs. However, I do suggest that these beneficiaries were too few in number to start that groundswell of opposition to proposed cuts in federal, state, and other spending on these programs. Part of the reason for this is that we were so intent on making sure that minority students got every service that was available to them, regardless of quality or effectiveness, that we never widened the political base that would have protected and supported these programs.

More than anything else, I believe, we needed then and must strive mightily now to ensure that such programs are seen as an investment in effective educational programming and not as a restricted resource with a sign reading "for minority students only."

Reagan administration officials, legislators, taxpayers, and college and university presidents have every right to demand that tax dollars generate a return on their investment. If we are not able to describe these returns in language that is clear to everyone and measure these returns by standards that all of us—minority and nonminority alike—agree are appropriate, then I believe our critics will be justified in claiming that there are other priorities that need attention and dollars more.

This means that we cannot tolerate high-cost programs for the educationally disadvantaged if they do not meet reasonable standards of achievement. We simply cannot continue to turn out graduates who cannot read at the same level of competence as their "advantaged" counterparts. This means that we cannot afford to perpetuate the notion that there are two agendas for higher education: one for the educationally disadvantaged and one for the nondisadvantaged. As long as this notion is allowed to persist, college and university officials will be justified in thinking that someone else must be found to pay the costs of keeping an add-on EO program afloat. Therefore, programs for the educationally disadvantaged must be integral to the mission of institutions of higher education.

We can help ourselves in this regard by correcting the third of the mistakes I alluded to earlier: namely, we can learn to do more with the resources we currently command. In too many instances programs for the educationally disadvantaged exist at institutions side by side with other programs that have, for all intents and purposes, the same educational goals and objectives. Thus, on many campuses there are separate reading skills programs for EOP and non-EOP students, carried on separate budget lines.

The problem is that these programs are supposed to do essentially the same things. All too frequently there are real differences in the expected outcomes of the programs, and, furthermore, the disadvantaged programs are more likely to employ minority personnel than the non-EO programs. We have perpetuated this duplication of effort in educational jargon. We use arguments suggesting that disadvantaged minority students can learn only when "one of their own" provides the academic support services. We further complicate matters by suggesting that, as a result, the EOP effort cannot be evaluated using the same criteria as other programs or that EOP students should not be expected to show the same progress toward the attainment of requisite academic competencies. In a rather pervasive and insidious manner, we allow the existence of an institutionalized double standard. It places an underprepared or unprepared student in an even more difficult academic position, where, if failure is not inevitable, it certainly is probable—especially in the marketplace.

My point, of course, is that we simply cannot have it both ways: we cannot expect any budget-minded administrator or legislator to continue to pay more for less, and especially when educationally disadvantaged students have to adjust subsequently to unfulfilled expectations. This is particularly true when we present two budgets—one for the EO program and one for the non-EO program—when it is all too obvious that there may not be enough dollars to support *one* program adequately. Doing a better job with the resources we have at hand means cleaning our own house before we ask someone else to help us pay the rent.

I like to think of myself as a realist. I became confirmed in this faith the day I became the president of a university in which the majority of the students are minority.

I did not forget on that day that this is still a racist society. I did not forget oppression. I did not forget the City of East St. Louis, which taught me the facts of life. I didn't forget the stupendous odds many of my students had to overcome simply to complete enough years of education to arrive at my institution. I didn't forget on that day that many of my students would face lives of hopelessness and despair should they fail to complete their education. I just could not discover how any of these facts was going to pay the bills. I could not, in other words, discover how continuing to refine and sharpen my analysis of the problem was going to pay for the solutions.

But that, I fear, is what too many of us are about. Describing how the system works in the 1980s can generate some marvelous prose, but—and I'm going to say it again and again—it doesn't pay the bills. Laying our problems at the feet of the current administration in Washington will not pay the bills either.

I have tried to suggest that the contemporary realist is one who accepts the responsibility of doing more and more with less and less. The realist is the person who gets paid to solve the problem, not one who becomes more articulate in describing it.

I want to propose, therefore, that we become realists in attempting to define the role of government in postsecondary programs for the educationally disadvantaged. The realist will tell you that even if minority folk were running the government, they would have one devil of a time trying to meet the demands of all the interest groups that lay special claim to some portion of tax revenues. The realist will tell you further that the only way to spend tax resources rationally is to demand that those dollars go to enterprises that bring some measurable and meaningful return on the investment.

Adopting this philosophy requires that we think like business people who have a product that must be marketed. The best marketing technique, it seems to me, is one that demonstrates that our product satisfies some important needs and meets critical performance standards. Since national economic productivity is a major issue today, perhaps we need to see what we have to offer to the investor who wants to support the solution to the problem of increasing national productivity.

In this regard, a report issued by the National Science Foundation and the U.S. Department of Education, *Science and Engineering Education in the 80's,* suggests that the key to future productivity lies in increasing the numbers of engineers and scientists and in developing greater literacy in matters pertaining to science and technology among all our citizens.

This report indicates that the United States is losing its position as a world leader in science and technology because it cannot match the output of a Japan or a West Germany in developing workers and researchers who can function in a postindustrial, highly technical and complex world. This is particularly true of minority groups who comprise less than 5 percent of all the scientists and engineers who are working at their craft in the United States.

Minority students, however, will comprise an ever-increasing portion of the 18-to-24-year-old population from which colleges traditionally draw students. Simple arithmetic will tell you that a major portion of new scientists and engineers *must* come from the ranks of minority students who comprise a growing and still largely untapped national resource. Most of us agree, furthermore, that programs for the educationally disadvantaged are of key importance in tapping this resource.

Such programs, however, at present do not have much to show in the way of developing this resource. A casual glance at EOP enrollments will reveal that a preponderance of students is enrolled in the social sciences and in education. Another glance will reveal that the traditionally black colleges do a lot better, on the average, in turning out scientists, engineers, and researchers. The truth of the matter is that enrollments in the hard sciences among EOP students have not changed greatly over the past decade and, if anything, are likely to go down, because students in general have been avoiding mathematics and science in the high schools and the junior high schools much more often today than 20 years ago.

I am not about to suggest that we develop a new program (or set of programs) specifically to address this issue. That habit comes too quickly to us. It is the kind of reasoning that says that every time you discover or can prove the existence of a "new" problem, a new program ought to be created. I'm of the belief that educational programs must be dynamic if they are to be responsive to changing societal needs. We are in an era of scarcity, and some cutting back and redesigning are inevitable. Furthermore, there is no profit, I maintain, in behaving as if the loss of even one program or one student would signal some cosmic tragedy. In truth, we have been neglecting some necessary quality control in many programs for too long.

Now, I suggest, is a time marked by the necessity to make adjustments, while the decision to do so is still ours to make! We can do this, for example, by requiring that programs enter into agreements with their host institutions to increase the flow of students into math- and science-oriented disciplines. There has to be an educational strategy that undergirds programs for the disadvantaged—a strategy that is grounded in a pragmatic assessment of need and opportunity. Acquainting our students with the facts of the marketplace and guiding them into the challenging areas of the curriculum are ultimately justified if we manage to reverse the disadvantaged minority student's continuing flight from mathematics and science.

Our primary goal should be to provide the type of educational opportunity that will give minority students increased access to the critical decision centers of the American social order. We must continually ask ourselves, therefore, if we are indeed providing useful and effective educational services and, if so, by what standards and with what goals. We must also question whether we are maintaining standards that are high enough and goals that demand the best we can provide. In these programs especially, we can no longer afford to offer educational services that are not demonstrably effective!

Those of you who thought immediately on hearing this: "Our students aren't prepared for that kind of course of study," or, "Our students would never survive in a mathematics and science program," are essentially admitting that your programs have little value in preparing students for the real world, a high-technology world.

Those of you who thought of how few of our students arrive at college prepared to undertake even high school algebra are hitting closer to the real issues, but if you also thought that the instruction high schools provide our students isn't your problem, you, too, are leaving your survival and that of your programs to someone else.

One of our most glaring failures, I believe, has been our unwillingness to demand high standards of performance from our students. I maintain that the biggest disservice inflicted on our youth is not the possible cutback in the programs that service them, but rather is our failure to demand—and obtain in return—the best they have to give. We are much too quick to point the finger of blame for substandard performance at society, the political structure, the economy, discrimination, or poorly prepared teachers. As a consequence, students have become quite glib at excusing themselves from any hard work.

At all levels of the education system, disadvantaged minority youth need assistance in setting higher expectation levels commensurate with their abilities and their commitment to sacrifice and hard work. We can help them by not accepting anything from each of them but their best, and we can help them by restraining our impulse to do it for them or to make excuses for their failures.

Does this sound as if I'm making the victims responsible for their condition? The answer is a resounding "yes" if responsibility in this context means making the victims responsible for their own salvation. They cannot look to others to do for them what they need to do for themselves. But we do have an important role in helping them with expanding their vision of their potential.

Yes, I can accept a reduced, perhaps even a nonexistent federal role in programs for the educationally disadvantaged as an inevitable consequence of this era of scarcity. What I've tried to suggest is that this only signals the end of narrowly defined roles and responsibilities. No resources will be generated by articulate condemnations of politicians and legislative leaders. We have work to do, and time is running out. Assume the worst: assume that we are on our own, assume that we have no one but ourselves and . . . welcome to the real world.

Response by Stephen Adolphus

I need to thank Jim Rosser for having risen to an occasion he didn't expect and giving us a powerful paper on very short notice. In my remarks I will concentrate on those areas in which I have somewhat alternative views and wish to present different perspectives.

First, Jim, it's not the "existential disequilibrium" (by which, I take it, you mean, "We're in trouble right now") that brought about this conference. It was rather the need, no matter what external forces impact on us, to look back at more than a decade of a concerted national effort—which we once thought might be a short-term effort—to take stock, to look ahead, to learn from our mistakes, and to try to provide for ourselves and others the best guidance we could for the years to come.

I hear again in Jim's paper the notion that "remediation quietly resulted in the lowering of expectations and standards." I think I see an essential non sequitur here. The logic in that statement is roughly, "Having to have remediation means students at our colleges are less well-prepared. That means admissions requirements were changed, lowered. That means the college is less good." Now, why is it less good? Simply because it has allowed in different people? Has the college lowered its graduation requirements because it instituted remediation? I think, usually, no. The point of remediation was to make sure that it *maintained* the graduation requirements. If colleges lowered their graduation requirements, what was the remediation about? If they didn't lower the graduation requirements, the only difference (provided one doesn't believe that providing remediation is *ipso facto* degrading) is that some people who might look different from students we used to have, and who need some more time to reach the same academic level, are now here. Unless you disagree with Ben Bloom, who has been invoked earlier at this conference, who suggests that people learn at different rates but that virtually all can learn, then there is nothing intrinsically standard-lowering in programs of remediation or developmental education. So I disagree.

Jim says that the programs want a handout, but the students don't do as much work as they should for it. I understand there's a certain amount of hyperbole here in order to make a case. But I'm not sure that giving up the time after your high school senior year to start college in the summer, attending regular and often compulsory tutoring sessions during the academic year, doing extra remedial work (often for no credit), having to take more time than your age cohort and peers to complete a college education, and often coming out of college with more loans because of the extra time are any indication of a break, or are somehow giving educational opportunity students more than the others get—just the contrary. It seems to me that they are assuming an extra burden.

Jim comments that there would have been more political success for the kind of programs we're addressing here if there had been a greater spill-over effect to other needy populations in colleges, and I think that this deserves serious consideration. It's a good point. As Ed Gordon and others have pointed out, many of these programs have been fiscally undercapi-talized even for their initial populations, much less for any new populations. Even so, one effect we've seen over time in federal, state, and institutional programs is the extending of services to others who need them before we've taken care of the first population, a rip-off effect, if you will. The extension of TRIO program eligibility in recent years is a case in point. Sometimes program staff will work double hours to take care of everybody who needs their help—especially at institutions in which categorically funded programs cannot cover all the students eligible for the services.

Then there is the ostrich effect. By this I mean institutional resistance to the notion that students *other* than "traditionally" disadvantaged or minority students need help. There are faculties who just can't adjust to the fact that "mainstream" kids can't read, write, and do arithmetic. There is less of that now than there used to be, but for a long time there was the unwill-ingness to face the fact that other populations needed support—especially academic support—and to mount the remedial and other programs needed.

Third, there was the suspicion, once the faculties recognized that students in the general population needed help, that minority staff couldn't deliver support services effectively to anyone but minority students, and a tendency for the majority population to bring in new kinds of developmental spe-cialists, a phenomenon we see all over the country. That's not to say there haven't been tremendously successful spill-over or umbrella programs on many campuses, building on the good knowledge and the pioneering of the special or opportunity programs to build up larger umbrella programs for other populations.

And just a note of caution in this regard: As we move in the direction of expanding educational opportunity program services to a broader popula-tion, attention and sensitivity are needed to make sure that the important role these programs play—providing special advocacy and an emotional home or focus for minorities on predominantly white campuses—is not diluted. This is a role that we don't know how to talk about very rationally.

I understand Jim's criticisms of the failure of many of our programs to set and to live up to reasonable academic standards. It may be true in some cases. Especially in the early days, when it was so hard to secure any resources or credibility, there was some fear on the part of program people to look at themselves too closely or to subject students to too much outside scrutiny—fear even to keep very complete records, because those records might be misinterpreted or used to harm the programs. However, the federal government must share some blame in this regard, especially concerning programs such as Special Services for Disadvantaged Students. As I see it, there has been an unwillingness ever really to collect systematically the kind of tough data on grades, on cohort survival over the college career (especially needed), and on placement after college that would allow real accountability for different programs, including a better basis for distribution of what are in fact very limited funds. This is a cop-out. It's almost as though there were a plan to set up these programs for criticism—the kind of criticism we just heard.

Next, I'm not convinced that demonstrating a tangible return (by which I gather Jim means a dollar return) on investments is the only way to justify federal tax revenue expenditures, even though the best of these programs are highly cost-effective compared to the alternative, which is unemployed, undereducated, and disaffected young people. Voting rights legislation, laws against crimes of violence, support for the arts, the national park system, and even the salaries of people who fly flags over the Capitol so that members of Congress can send them home to constituents don't require economic rationales—by which I mean to say that the federal government serves a number of purposes, not all of which can be measured in direct dollar returns. Among those purposes is the moral leadership of the country, a responsibility it can abrogate for any length of time only at its peril. Unless we are willing to say we want to return to a loose confederation of quasi-autonomous states, we must look to the center, to the federal government, for those things that hold us together, all resting on a Constitutional framework and certain broad and deep principles.

With regard to educational opportunity, the federal role has to continue to be to exert pressure toward full enfranchisement of all of our people—perhaps not in every administration and in every economic circumstance through providing big bucks, but always insisting on some movement toward the results we need and must have. The reluctance of recent Congresses and recent administrations to face up to moral issues in certain social areas and to rely on the federal courts to do the right thing is not acceptable. We cannot allow ourselves to count on a politically appointed judiciary as the only salvation.

If political pressure is to be one of the outcomes of gatherings like this, I think it should be used first to remind the federal government of its responsibility as the ultimate guarantor of human rights in this country. For if we leave this arena to the states, the localities, and the institutions, we will be sure of very uneven and many times pernicious results.

Mao Tse-Tung, who has been quoted earlier by Ed Gordon, said in addition to his theory of contradictions that we must battle on many fronts at the same time. This is not to say, then, that the states are off the hook simply because we must hold the federal government's feet to the fire.

These are times, clearly, when there is a lessening of the federal presence in education generally and in educational opportunity particularly. Thus it is important that the same skill and intensive lobbying effort at the federal level that proponents of higher education opportunity, exemplified by Arnie Mitchum and others in this room, have learned over the last 20 years on behalf of the disadvantaged, must be broadened to include a state focus— with dollars where possible, but always with the moral suasion, coordination, sanctions, and leadership that government at its very best can bring us.

Editor's note:

The room erupted when Rosser finished. While the agenda called for our moving to smaller groups for discussion, everyone clearly wanted to stay put, since, as one participant said, "We've come for a barbecue, and here is where the barbecuee is."

Much of the debate centered on a general disagreement with the speaker's contention that the special programs are adequately capitalized—a point he reinforced in the discussion. Participants raised such examples as the disparity in per capita funding between community colleges (where the majority of disadvantaged students are) and four-year institutions and challenged Rosser's understanding of the reality of special-interest group funding.

Rosser further elaborated his position, claiming the real flaw in the system was that educational opportunity students do not receive sufficient support from "mainstream" activities. In turn, the special sources set up to compensate for these lacks are a drain on institutional resources. Many in the audience found this line of reasoning unacceptable, insisting that the mainstreaming of special programs anytime soon was an illusory ideal, leaving few alternatives to reliance on public, and especially federal, funding.

The discussion, which was at a high pitch at this point, moved on to what someone called "the myth of giving it back to the states," the point being that, in a complex society, the central government must always be the responsible agency for ensuring that people are not mistreated. The idea that the administration was looking for "a return on its investment" was examined in light of proposed reductions in such proven programs as Title I of the Elementary and Secondary Education Act.

The "quality" issue surfaced here. One reactor suggested that the "objective" instruments that the postsecondary community so heavily relies on to validate quality are in fact used to degrade people. Several brought out the theme of "don't blame the victims for things over which they have no control"—i.e., the federal economy and the higher education establishment. It was agreed that some concessions had had to be made to get special equity programs off the ground, but that there was no need now to apologize, to "self-flagellate." A participant pointed out that the argument in the end is not about equality, but sufficiency to reach such goals as quality. Extrapolating from elementary and secondary education, he estimated the current national need to be double the resources available.

Finally, using as an example the black teacher who teaches badly to black students, Rosser said we must be much clearer and more honest about what the situation is and specify more exactly what our goals are, before we can make the best use of the resources available or mount convincing arguments for increased support.

The Connection between Postsecondary Programs for the Disadvantaged and Elementary and Secondary Schools

Barbara A. Sizemore

During these pressing times, when the president of the United States advocates the achievement of fiscal solvency through the elimination of programs for the needy, it seems to me most urgent that we address the most important problems of the constituency served: the problem of access to postsecondary education and to employment opportunities, since these are the most threatened by the administration's thrust.

Postsecondary educational programs for the disadvantaged are mainly concerned with recruitment, remediation, and retention. Such programs interface with elementary and secondary schools in several places: (1) in the accreditation and evaluation of elementary and secondary schools; (2) in the establishment of standards for high school graduation and college admissions; (3) in the design of courses for elementary and high school students; (4) in the implementation of remedial and compensatory programs for college freshmen or high school seniors; (5) in the preparation of elementary and secondary school teachers; (6) in the counseling of high school students; (7) through research efforts in educational institutions; (8) through consultancies and advisory commissions; (9) through the communications media; and (10) through court decrees, legislation, and governmental intervention. This paper will discuss the connections with secondary and elementary schools that serve the black poor.

First, an attempt will be made to review briefly the history of black education in the United States and to argue the position that governmental intervention is imperative if justice is to be served. Second, a review of the research relating to effective schooling will be presented. Third, a discussion of the effects of Reaganomics on black education will be given. Finally, some recommendations for the future will be offered.

Most postsecondary programs for the disadvantaged result from governmental intervention. An example is the Higher Education Equal Opportunity Program (Act 101), established in Pennsylvania in 1971, which encourages institutions of higher learning to admit low-income students, who, because of poor performance on standardized tests, inadequate high school preparation, or both would not normally be admitted. These institutions recruit highly motivated students who show the potential to succeed in college with adequate support (counseling, tutoring, and financial assistance). The goal of Act 101 is to help the institutions provide opportunities for nontraditional students seeking a college education. Act 101 programs offer the right kind of support services and survival skills for students, male and female, young and old, in 53 institutions throughout Pennsylvania.

Governmental intervention has been required in the United States to combat institutional racism, which had spawned a two-tiered school system—one for whites and one for blacks.

History of Black Education in the United States

The educational history of African Americans can be divided into seven approximate periods, which overlap: (1) the Pre-Columbian Exploration Period, ending in 1492; (2) the period of the Afro-European Explorations, ending in 1619; (3) the period of Slavery, ending in 1865; (4) the period of the First Reconstruction, ending in 1896; (5) the period of the First Jim Crow, ending in 1954; (6) the period of the Second Reconstruction, ending in 1974; and (7) the period of the Second Jim Crow, in which we are now living. Racism is the expression of one race's superiority to another in a culture. Institutional racism is the legalization of that expression and its translation into rules, standards, norms, and customs. Reconstruction is the name applied to those eras in the history of black education when the United States attempted to rebuild the social order by mitigating those rules, norms, and customs and by redressing deprivations caused by their institutionalization. Jim Crow refers to the legislation and practice that separate the races and mark whites as superiors and blacks as inferiors.

There have always been free black men in the United States. These men struggled to educate their people in the schools that they established. The Pittsburgh African Education Society was formed on January 16, 1832, and stated in the preamble of its constitution that "ignorance is the sole cause of the present degradation of the people of color in the United States." They empowered a board of managers to purchase books, raise money, acquire land, and erect suitable buildings to accommodate instruction. Actually, the board of managers acted as a school board and initiated a successful school operation.[1] But for the masses of black people after 1619 slavery was the norm, and education was prohibited by the Black Codes— laws restricting the movement, education, and rights of African-Americans. They could not learn to read, write, or compute nor own the earnings of their own labor, land, or family. Consequently, when slavery ended, these people had no means by which they could care for themselves and their families.

On March 3, 1865, before the Civil War ended, the federal government established an agency, the Bureau of Refugees, Freedmen and Abandoned Lands, commonly referred to as the Freedmen's Bureau, in the War Department to oversee the large number of former slaves following the Union Army in search of employment, food, and help. This agency was responsible for establishing schools for the refugees. DuBois describes the agency's efforts in this way.

> The insistent demand of the Negro, aided by army officers and Northern churches and philanthropic organizations, began the systematic teaching of Negroes and poor whites. This beginning the Freedmen's Bureau raised to a widespread system of Negro public schools. The Bureau furnished day and night schools, industrial schools, Sunday schools and colleges. Between June 1, 1865, and September 1, 1871, $5,262,511.26 was spent on schools from Bureau funds and in 1870 there were in day and night schools 3,300 teachers and 149,581 pupils. Nearly all the present Negro universities and colleges like Howard, Fisk and Atlanta, were founded or substantially aided in their earliest days by the Freedmen's Bureau.[2]

In fact, it was the press for education by the former slaves that initiated and accelerated the growth of the public school system in the former Confederate States.

Prior to the abolition of slavery, public schools did not exist in the South except for North Carolina. DuBois explains this phenomenon.

> The fact of the matter was that in the pre-war South, there were two insuperable obstacles to a free public school system. The first was the attitude of the owners of property. They did not propose under any circumstances to be taxed for the public education of the laboring class. They believed that laborers did not need an education; that it made their exploitation more difficult; and that if any of them were really worth educating, they would somehow escape their condition by their own effort. The second obstacle was that the white laborers did not demand education, and saw no need of it, save in exceptional cases. It was only the other part of the laboring class, the black folk who connected knowledge with power; who believed that education was the stepping-stone to wealth and respect, and that wealth, without education, was crippled.[3]

During the Reconstruction the newly formed state governments, many of them with black representatives, started public schools. But opposition to the education of the Negro remained strong, and the Negro school system was saved by Northern philanthropy rather than Southern enlightenment.[4]

This Northern support, and its attempt to transplant the New England college to the South and to give the former slaves a leadership based on scholarship and character, is considered the salvation of the black man, who "would have rushed into revolt and vengeance and played into the hands of those determined to crush him."[5] Eighty-four normal schools and high schools and 16 colleges with over 12,000 students were formed. These eventually became the centers of training for the black middle class and its leadership—which, when reaction triumphed in 1876, were already present to guide the black people through the terror.[6]

The struggle for the 14th and 15th Amendments to the Constitution and the supporting enforcement legislation such as the Civil Rights Act of 1875 evoked a storm of racism and installed white supremacy as the legacy of the First Reconstruction. By the time of the 1876 Presidential election the abolitionists' influence had diminished in the Republican Party, which was forced to negotiate with three former Confederate States—South Carolina, Louisiana, and Florida—in order to win the fiercely contested election. In return for the congressional votes to certify the Republican slate of presidential electors in these contested states, Hayes promised, as president, to withdraw all federal troops from the South, leaving the black man unprotected against the brutal terrorism of the Ku Klux Klan and the Knights of the White Camelia, and to guarantee the interest payment on a massive bond issue by the Texas and Pacific Railroad.[7]

After the withdrawal of the military, the Southern states immediately began to enforce Jim Crow legislation with a fury, denying the black man his newly won rights. In 1883 the Supreme Court declared the Civil Rights Act of 1875 unconstitutional. This legislation had been the first to protect the civil, social, and political rights of the black man. The 1875 Act "asserted that all people regardless of race or color were guaranteed the full and equal enjoyment of the accommodations . . . of inns, public conveyances on land and water, theatres and other places of public amusement and that no one was to be disqualified for jury service because of race, color or previous condition of servitude."[8] Sumner of Massachusetts guided this bill through the Congress but failed to have unsegregated schools included among the rights therein guaranteed. In 1896 the Supreme Court handed down its decision in the case of Plessy *versus* Ferguson, legalizing Jim Crow practice and bringing the First Reconstruction era to a close.

Homer Adolph Plessy was a light-skinned octoroon and a Louisiana citizen, who had refused to leave a seat in a white coach of a railroad train for one in the black coach, in compliance with the Louisiana law of equal but separate accommodations for the white and colored races of that state. The Supreme Court ruled against Plessy, denying his pleas that his 14th Amendment rights had been violated by the law and upholding the use of police power to deny equal protection of the laws.[9] In this decision the Supreme Court accepted the doctrine of "separate but equal accommodations," justifying this clearly unjust action in this way.

> We consider the underlying fallacy of the plaintiff's argument to consist in the assumption that the enforced separation of the two races stamps the colored race with a badge of inferiority. If this be so, it is not by reason of anything found in the act, but solely because the colored race chooses to put that construction upon it.[10]

Thus, in Kluger's words, the Supreme Court Justices "had tortured truth to make the shoe fit." For the black man there was no justice, and racism was now legalized by the last word in American law, the Supreme Court. The black man had no rights that a white man need honor. This legal interpretation prevailed for 58 years. The practice continued for nearly 10 years more.

With this understanding of the history of black education, the race problem in the United States can be studied as a struggle for human, civil, social, and political rights rather than one of race relations. Jim Crow was more than a problem in race relations. It was the denial of the rights of black citizens. During the slavery era the struggle was more basic—one of human rights, which are the rights of life, liberty, and the pursuit of happiness. The 13th Amendment protected the human rights of black people. With the passing of the 14th Amendment blacks became citizens, and the Constitution protected their civil rights—the right to free speech, assembly, and religion; to bear arms; to freedom of thought and faith; to own and defend one's property; to conclude contracts; and to justice. The 15th Amendment guaranteed their political rights—the right to vote and to hold political office. Consequently, during the first Jim Crow period the struggle was against the steady erosion of these human, civil, and political rights. This struggle ended in the now famous Brown *versus* Topeka Supreme Court case decided on May 17, 1954, insuring equality of education. Here the social rights of black people were insured. Social rights are those assuring economic welfare and security, education, and the right to share in the social heritage as a civilized being according to the standards prevailing in the social order.

Neither the problem of slavery nor Jim Crow was a problem of one race relating to another. It was a case in which a race that considered itself superior to another deprived the one designated as inferior of certain basic rights guaranteed by the Constitution and democratic practice and norms. The redress of all of these prior deprivations and the attainment of equal status as citizens of the United States became the twin goals of the Second Reconstruction following the 1954 Supreme Court Decision. Some researchers say that the mistake made during this era was the consideration of Jim Crow as the problem rather than institutionalized racism.[11]

Jim Crow laws were the supreme manifestation of institutionalized racism. Although the Supreme Court in Plessy *versus* Ferguson had condoned Jim Crow, conditions had to be equal. The reality, however, was that racism prohibited equality. Black people were denied the right to homestead, to enter organized labor, to compete on an equal basis for even demeaning jobs, to vote, and to get an equal education. Jim Crow made this denial legal. These laws were enforced by terrorist organizations, and equal protection was never afforded. Therefore, the deprivation of the rights of black people was not a coincidence or an unexpected quirk of events. It was planned, legalized, and judged fair and just by the highest tribunal of the land. Government intervention created the condition in which the black man would be inferior and kept him that way. It was only logical and natural, then, for the black man to look to the government for redress. This effort finally culminated in the Supreme Court's judgment in Brown *versus* Topeka in 1954, bringing the period of the First Jim Crow to a close.

The uphill struggle to overturn Plessy *versus* Ferguson emerged in the 1940s, with cases from Clarendon County, South Carolina; Farmville, Virginia; Washington, D.C.; and Topeka, Kansas, and the latter became the lead case in the litigation. Since it was highly unlikely that the Supreme Court would reverse its decision in Plessy for the human, civil, social, or political rights of a black man, the plaintiff had to be carefully chosen and the issue of contention had to be as innocuous as possible. No case could have met these requirements better than the fight to secure equal educational opportunity for a little black girl. Hence, the National Association for the Advancement of Colored People (NAACP) chose as its flagship case that of Oliver Brown *versus* the Topeka Board of Education. Oliver Brown was litigating on behalf of his daughter, Linda Brown, who was seven years old at that time.

Linda Brown had to walk between train tracks for half a dozen blocks to catch the school bus to the segregated school that she attended. Fed up with this dangerous route, Oliver Brown took her to register at the all-white school several blocks away from their home. She was denied admission. The case reached the Supreme Court on December 9, 1952:

> . . . fifty-six years after segregation was approved in Plessy, ninety years after the Emancipation Proclamation, 163 years after the ratification of the Constitution,

and 333 years after the first African slave was known to have been brought to the shores of the New World, the Supreme Court convened to hear arguments on whether the white people of the United States might continue to treat the black people as their subjects.[12]

From 1619 to 1865 black people had been slaves. From 1865 to 1954 they had been second-class citizens. The Supreme Court Decision of May 17, 1954, in favor of Oliver Brown commuted this sentence to second-class citizenship and began the quest for equal status and redress for these prior deprivations.

Jim Crow did not die an easy death. Custom and tradition sought to keep the practice institutionalized. Nonviolent direct action, riots, and rebellion were directed toward its elimination. The government intervened with (1) legislation to safeguard the rights of black people to vote, to use public conveyances and facilities, and to have equal employment opportunities; (2) affirmative action to redress the prior deprivation of exclusion from these jobs; (3) open admissions to expand access to higher education; (4) a more democratic multi-ethnic curriculum in schools, to teach the history, literature, and culture of black people; and (5) more programs directed toward the mitigation of the exigencies of poverty.

In 1972 Richard M. Nixon won the presidency on a platform of reaction and white backlash for (1) more law and order; (2) a restoration of states' rights; (3) the appointment of strict constructionists to the Supreme Court; (4) a reduction in poverty programs; and (5) the benign neglect of black human, civil, social, and political rights. The fight against busing for school integration led to a movement for a Constitutional amendment to ban it. In 1974 the Supreme Court handed down its decision in Bakke *versus* the University of California Medical School at Davis. In this petition Allen Paul Bakke, a white man, charged the University of California with reverse discrimination pleading that his 14th Amendment rights had been abridged by the denial of his petition to be admitted to the Medical School while 16 spaces were reserved for minorities less qualified than he. Antibusing and reverse discrimination became the new cries for the retreat from the guarantees of equal status and redress for prior deprivation.

The original position of reverse discrimination was posited by President Andrew Johnson in his speech against the passage of the Civil Rights Bill of 1866. He said that the law establishes "for the security of the colored race safeguards which go infinitely beyond any that the general government have ever provided for the white race," and therefore discriminated against the white race.[13] His logic did not consider the fact that the black man's treatment in slavery went infinitely far beyond any treatment that the general government had legalized against the white race. In 1974 there was a widespread feeling among the citizens that African Americans had arrived and now needed no more favoritism. This feeling proved to be the harbinger of the return of Jim Crow.

At the same time the economy was shrinking, the gross national product was slipping, the budget deficit was widening, and inflation was growing by leaps and bounds. The major industries were losing money. Blue collar workers especially were losing their jobs, and this high unemployment disproportionately affected blacks. They became disillusioned with the slow rate of progress of desegregation in improving the quality of education of their children in both desegregated and segregated schools, and quality education evolved as their highest priority.

They began to ask why excellence could not exist in all black schools. There have always been schools in which black and/or poor students have demonstrated high achievement as determined by standardized test scores;[14] however, these schools have been the exception rather than the rule. More often, inner-city schools, as they are known, have languished at the bottom when ranked by achievement with other schools in the same system.[15] The high-achieving predominantly black school remains an abashing anomaly, which frequently embarrasses responsible school officials who do not often invite comparisons that raise questions about the ineffectiveness of large numbers of other predominantly black schools where the majority of the students are low-achieving.

Many explanations have been given for black underachievement as a group phenomenon. Whatever belief system provokes the assumptions in a study also influences the results of the research. The results, then, structure designs for social reform. Following are five main categories of beliefs from which cause statements have evolved.

- Blacks are genetically inferior in intelligence.[16]
- Blacks are culturally deprived, or their cultural conflicts prevent their learning.[17]
- Blacks' families, homes, and community environments are deficient, indifferent, unstimulating, and immoral.[18]
- The school and/or school system are/is inefficient, underfunded, and ineffective.[19]
- The larger social order dictates through its value system a racial caste/class system that perpetuates itself through the schools.[20]

Since racially isolated black schools have been discovered in which students score at or above the national norms in reading and mathematics on standardized achievement tests, the first three beliefs could not apply to these schools. This contradiction caused many researchers to search for effective black schools and to study the reasons for this aberration. It seemed important that responsible educators and interested people should know that public schools could be effective in elevating achievement among the black poor and that the means could be efficient.

The political struggle around desegregation and decentralization obstructed substantial efforts to eliminate the undereachievement of black and/or poor students and the reviewed research revealed the following aftereffects.

1. Racially isolated schools remained even after schools districts had desegregated.

2. Many metropolitan urban areas where large numbers of poor blacks live had not yet desegregated, a full 28 years after Brown.

3. In many desegregated school districts whites have fled the public schools leaving a majority black public school system.

4. The elevation of achievement in desegregated school settings was often as difficult to achieve as in their segregated counterparts.

5. The side effects of inadequate desegregation practices further institutionalized racism in the public school system.[21]

Errors in desegregation policy and strategy are, as stated before, according to some theorists, due to the assumption that Jim Crow and not racism was the evil. As a result of these errors, desegregation models developed into quota systems for race balancing, instead of paradigms for equal status and the redress of prior deprivation. Generally, desegregation practices stressed the following.

1. White majorities, preferably 80/20.

2. One-way busing, blacks only.

3. Closing of black schools.

4. Placement of blacks in groups by testing.

5. Increased remedial and compensatory programs for blacks.

6. More facilities and staff or special education, primarily for the mentally retarded and the socioemotionally disturbed.

7. The firing or demotion of black staff.

8. An increased use of exit testing for students and entry testing for teachers.[22]

Some blacks became impatient with the slow progress made in desegregation and were frustrated by the lack of improvement in the quality of education in their neighborhood schools. As a result, they pressed for community control. Their contention was that they could acquire a better education for their children if they could make the policy for the institutions that affect the children.[23] The community control movement peaked with the Ocean Hill–Brownsville controversy in New York City, but the New York City teachers' strike of 1968 heralded the decline of this option for the black community. Although several cities experimented with various forms of decentralization, the policymaking powers envisioned by the initiators of the movement rarely materialized. Under decentralization, the authority of the central office administration was delegated to area or district officials in some cases, and, in others, the central board shared some of its powers with local boards. But, generally, decentralized units could not hire or fire or negotiate with the unions.[24] Nor did decentralization bring about a noticeable change in achievement in predominantly black, poor schools.

In 1966 James S. Coleman produced his extensive study, *Equality of Educational Opportunity,* commissioned by Section 402 of the 1964 Civil Rights Act.[25] The major finding was that public schools did not greatly affect learning and that the most important variable was the family background of the students. However, buried in the report there was also the observation that the achievement of minority pupils depended more on the schools they attended than did the achievement of majority pupils.[26] Not much attention was given to the report between 1966 and 1971, since the larger social order was disturbed by the community control movement, the big city riots, the Vietnam War reaction, and the assassinations of Martin Luther King, Jr., and John and Robert Kennedy.[27]

Many arguments pro and con were generated during the Nixon presidency, however, when Moynihan promoted his idea of benign neglect, which projected that "school reform was wasted on the poor, since only massive intervention in their lives would ameliorate the intrinsic disabilities from which they suffered."[28] During this time literature declaring the ineffectiveness and inefficiency of inner-city public schools proliferated[29] and was met by three oppositional streams: (1) the unions' response of "more effective schools"; (2) the black community's quest for community control and quality education; and (3) social scientists' research on black and poor schools. The unions' notion was based on the belief that schools could produce if the conditions were improved for teachers permitting them to spend more time on instruction and to make more decisions regarding their work conditions. The unions' "more effective schools" idea developed simultaneously with the press for quality education in northern, black, urban communities.[30]

Research on Effective Schools

In the early 1970s social scientists began to produce a growing body of data on effective schools. These data dealt with schools where children, black and poor, were learning. Strong leadership was one of the characteristics described. The principal of this kind of school was instrumental in setting the tone of the school, helping decide on instructional strategies, organizing and distributing the school's resources, bringing the disparate elements of the school together and developing a consensus among the school actors around high achievement as a goal for all the children in the school.[31]

Brookover and Lezotte, in contrast, found a principal in one declining school who was very much public-relations oriented and made a very strong effort to project a favorable image of the school. He praised his school as very good and exalted the cooperativeness and quality of his staff but provided no significant supervision and played a minor role in directing instructional activities. Teachers there tended to run their own show and to do what they wanted in the classroom. The principal in this declining school did not give a high priority to achievement in mathematics and reading—nor any basic skills.[32] Brookover and Lezotte summarized the consequences of such leadership.

> . . . (1) there are no achievement goals set and there is no evaluation of the level of mastery in math and reading; (2) there is a general rejection of any account-ability for student achievement; (3) the level of achievement is determined by non-school factors associated with the children and their parents and the home environment; the teachers, thus, have very low expectations and they assume no responsibility for successful teaching of math and reading.[33]

Lezotte and Passalacqua found that individual buildings accounted for a significant amount of the variance in measured pupil performance; how-ever, their research did not speak to the factors operating in the individual building.

Improving schools emphasize reading and mathematics goals and objec-tives, while declining schools give much less emphasis to them. Staffs in improving schools tend to believe that all of the students can learn, while the declining schools' teachers project the belief that the students' abilities are low and that they cannot master the objectives. Staffs in improving schools hold higher expectations for their students, while those in declining schools feel that their students will not finish high school or go on to college. Staff in improving schools take the responsibility for teaching the basic reading and mathematics skills, while those in declining schools tend to displace this responsibility on the parents or the students themselves. Improving schools spend more time on the basic skills than do declining schools. Their principals seem to be more assertive, more "take charge" types, more aggressive disciplinarians, and more likely to function as in-structional leaders. Principals in declining schools tend to be more permis-sive and to emphasize informal and collegial relationships with teachers. Teachers in improving schools are generally less satisfied than teachers in declining schools. There seems to be less overall parent involvement in the improving schools, although improving schools have a higher level of parent-initiated involvement, and improving schools are not characterized by a great emphasis on paraprofessional staff nor heavy involvement of regular teachers in the selection of students to be placed in compensatory education programs. The declining schools seem to have a greater number of different staff involved in reading instruction and more teacher involvement in identifying students who are to be placed in compensatory education programs.[34]

We do know some things to do in schools to elevate achievement. We need different routines for teachers and principals to follow in high-achieving schools. First, no principal should be assigned to a black or poor school who does not believe that the students there can learn. Second, principals must be committed to the goal of high achievement and must not substitute growth, good citizenship, or any other characteristic—no matter how worthy—for this goal. Teachers must be monitored in such a way that instruction leads to achievement. Skill mastery learning seems to be a most successful strategy at this time; however, we must be conscious of the future of computers in education and we must begin a more intelligent use of them in our curriculum. Mathematics is a necessity in the electronic age of the 21st century. We should require 12 years of mathematics as we now require 12 years of English. We should demand more rigorous study of science to prepare students for employment in a high-technology environment. This means more prospective teachers need to be turned on to mathematics and science in teacher-training institutions. High expectations must be held for student progress by principals and teachers, and these expectations must be enforced with routines that assist students to learn the necessary skills.

In high-achieving schools more time is often needed for students with prior deprivation and unequal status. This may mean future negotiations with teachers' unions for longer days in order to accommodate the entire curriculum, so that committed teachers need not steal time from music, art, social studies, and science in order to teach reading and mathematics. The use of Title I* funds for programming needs to be more innovative, so that students who need this service are not shortchanged in the regular instructional program.

Most important, the present dilemma of principals and administrators who are committed to high achievement must be alleviated. Now, these principals must often disagree with their superior officers on the implementation of certain routines that make schools low achieving, and at the same time arbitrate the discontent of students, parents, and teachers with the new routines that are necessary for the high-achieving school. Caught

---

*Now known as Chapter I.—*Ed.*

between a rock and a hard place, the principal committed to high achievement in a poor black school must risk classification by the central office as a poor team player. This classification removes promotion as a logical outcome of superior service. Additionally, the principal may alienate faculty and community with his or her new standards. Treading these dangerous waters should not be a requirement for changing a low-achieving school.

Institutions that prepare teachers must (1) raise the standards for the teaching of mathematics and science and train teachers to meet them and (2) provide an education for teachers in American history telling the story of the participation of all the people, not just the Europeans, complete with the contribution of black people to the greatness of the nation and showing the betrayal of these people by their own government, courts, and law enforcement agencies—all of which violated their human, civil, social, and political rights. At present, black history is a long train of vignettes about the lives of important black men and women. The concept of a struggle for denied rights and the presence of Africans in the New World before Columbus are rarely taught. As a result, African Americans appear as appendages to European exploits rather than integral parts of the history through their own acts of initiative. Teachers need a stronger multicultural base for music, art, literature, drama, poetry, and language. Most subjects are Eurocentric in their focus.

High school teachers need to be oriented toward students' needs as well as toward their subjects. Firestone and Herriott attempted to identify images of the social organization of elementary and secondary schools in their study.[35] The two images used were the rational bureaucracy and the natural system. The three conceptual domains used to distinguish the rational bureaucracy and the natural system were: goal consensus, centralization of control, and the extent of coordination. The authors found that the elementary schools were more like rational bureaucracies and high schools were more like natural systems. The rational bureaucracy was a formally organized social structure with clearly defined patterns of activities in which every series of actions was functionally related to the goals of the organization. Rationality came from interdependence of the system's parts, effective coordination, and firm enlightened administrators. By contrast, in the natural system, actions were not clearly related to goals. In fact, individual interests could substitute for goals as the primary motivating force. Then interdependence would be reduced and control would be dispersed. Since research on effective schools has shown that high-achievement goals are characteristic of high-achieving schools, the natural system routines of the high school should work against high achievement in reading and mathematics for the black poor learner.

In her analytic study of two desegregated junior high schools in 1967, Metz found that schools make choices among formal goals or exist with "managed or unmanaged conflict." She says:

> And they must reconcile the requirements of these formal goals with the require-
> ments of maintaining order among the students and support from the community,
> a task which . . . often requires sacrifices of the formal goals.[36]

In her study the problems that arose around achieving these goals seemed to be the lack of goal consensus among the teachers and between teachers and administrators, the lack of congruity between structure and goals, and the absence of mechanisms for communication among the actors in the institutions. Metz interpreted order as an instrumental goal or a means to achieve education. She did not consider order as a formal goal.[37]

Metz did point out, however, that principals had direct responsibility without direct control over the events for which they must answer. She interpreted the principals' responses as choices between two goals: to support and encourage diversity, experimentation and independence among both teachers and students, and to establish and maintain good order. For the accomplishment of the former goals, she felt, the school district gave the principals great autonomy in administering the school; but for the latter there was little support and few resources.[38]

In a review of the literature on effective schools Edmonds reported differences between low- and high-achieving schools in: (1) administrative behavior, policies, and practices; (2) management, instructional routines, and standard operating procedures; (3) teacher attitudes toward the students' abilities to learn; (4) teacher expectations for student performance; (5) amount of time spent in instructional activities; and (6) degree and quality of assistance given to teachers.[39] He ends his review with this comment:

> . . . whether or not we will ever effectively teach the children of the poor is
> probably far more a matter of politics than of social science and that is as it
> should be. It seems to me, therefore, that what is left of this discussion are three
> declarative statements. We can, whenever and wherever we choose, successfully
> teach all children whose schooling is of interest to us. We already know more
> than we need in order to do this. Whether we do it must finally depend on how
> we feel about the fact that we haven't so far.[40]

To be sure, the public school is a part of a vast political system where groups with vested interests war over scarce resources. These groups consist of parents, administrators, citizens and politicians, teachers, and students. Often their cause-and-effect beliefs do not match and are irreconcilable. In those cases, the poor usually wind up with the short end of the stick. This seems to be happening today.

The Effect of Reaganomics on Black Education

The attitude and policies of the present administration are effectively implementing a new kind of institutionalized racism through its economic and social programs aimed toward currying favor with the affluent and the conservative right, and dedicated to the separation of the races and the exploitation of the poor and helpless. The Reagan administration fosters and advocates the following programs which disproportionately limit the opportunities of the black poor: (1) the curtailment or elimination of educational programs targeted for the poor and/or disadvantaged; (2) the reduction or elimination of loans, grants, and social security benefits for the college-bound; (3) tuition tax credits and vouchers, which will be funded with 2.7 billion dollars taken from public schools; (4) the reduction of Title I monies and the threat to reduce Head Start, Upward Bound, and similar programs; (5) tax exemptions for institutions practicing racism, such as Bob Jones University; (6) constructive engagement with South Africa; (7) mandatory draft registration; (8) separate rules for political refugees from Haiti; (9) reduction of programs for Aid to Families with Dependent Children, such as food stamps; (10) the elimination of job training programs for youth, such as CETA; (11) the refusal of the Justice Department to protect the civil and social rights of black people in segregated environments; (12) the elimination of funding for the Neighborhood Legal Departments; (13) the denial of the rule of one man, one vote for blacks in voting districts; (14) a voting rights act that disregards the statistical results of gerrymandering but relies instead on proof of intent to discriminate; and (15) a system of federalism that is a throwback to the old states' rights position of John C. Calhoun, resurrected during the First Jim Crow era.

Reaganomics requires that fiscal solvency be reached by abolishing the entitlement programs that succor the poor. The effect of these administration positions is to negate the progress that African Americans have made since 1954. Poverty restricts opportunity unless governmental intervention redresses the prior deprivation caused by Jim Crow, which was in operation for 77 years. Affirmative action, open admissions, and entitlement programs have been available to African Americans for only 9 years—from 1965 through 1974. For example, the Pittsburgh Public Schools hired no black teachers in an integrated school system from 1874 to 1933.[41] From 1933 until 1962 the recruitment and hiring of black teachers was minimal. There were 105 black professonals in the Pittsburgh Public Schools in 1954 of a total professional staff of 2,577 or 4.1 percent. The bulk of the black personnel was hired between 1964 and 1977. Four hundred seventy black professionals were hired between those years, resulting in 771 or 19.4 percent.[42] Today, the Pittsburgh Board of Education is faced with a reduction in force due to low enrollment. With the application of seniority standards, black teachers will be dismissed disproportionately. They will pay twice for racist practices, unless there is governmental intervention to prevent this double jeopardy.

The 1980 census shows that 50.9 percent of Black Americans 25 years and older graduated from high school. With the advent of tougher college admissions requirements and the disappearance of government grants and of open admissions, the opportunities of blacks will evaporate in the hot caldron of racial discrimination based on prior deprivation, which has never been redressed because desegregation and the improvement of the quality of education in predominantly black schools were delayed, deferred, or ignored. Pittsburgh has been desegregating and in court since 1965.

Moreover, the economy of the country is weak and Reaganomics seeks to revitalize it on the backs of the poor, pitting blacks and whites against each other for the meager resources. John Kenneth Galbraith, speaking in the March 17, 1982, issue of *The New Republic* says:

> . . . in an economy with a strong tendency to inflation, there are only three countering lines of policy . . . (1) direct restraint on wages and prices in the highly organized sector; (2) restraint on inflation through budget reduction; and (3) the use of monetary policy as an agent against inflation.

He states that the Federal Reserve firmly refuses to allow money creation, and, therefore, a stern monetary policy has forced an increase in interest rates. Control over the money supply then restrains bank lending, bank deposit, and money creation. He further concludes that high interest rates curb spending through pricing credit beyond the reach of the potential borrowers and the consequences are:

> From the constraint imposed on lending come reduced spending for capital and consumer goods, a recession in economic activity, and, if not lower prices, at least a lessened rate of inflation. That has been the effect of the policy in the last months.

Many industries have succumbed to these practices, especially those dependent on borrowed money: automobile dealers, home builders, real estate brokers, farmers, and small business in general, where the failure rate last year reached the highest level, one year excepted, since the Great Depression. Galbraith warns that these are the consequences we must expect if budget deficits mandate a continued reliance on monetary policy as the alternative to severe inflation.

Reaganomics will not work, according to Galbraith. In the first place, he states that our expenditures on the poor have not been high in relation to the gross national product (GNP) in comparison with those of other major industrial countries. However, in contrast, our expenditures on the military have exceeded that of other countries. Through the 1970s our investment in fixed nonmilitary and nonresidential expenditures ranged from 16.9 percent of the GNP to 19 percent; that of West Germany ranged from 20.6 to 26 percent of the GNP; that of Japan, 31 percent to 36.6 percent. On the other hand, at the same time, 5 to 8 percent of the GNP of the United States was spent for military purposes, while West Germany spent 3 to 4 percent of its GNP and Japan less than 1 percent. Per capita, for the United States this amounts to $441; West Germany, $252; and Japan, $47.

Galbraith charges that it was the capital saved from military spending—from which a substantial share of the civilian investment came—that brought these countries to the industrial eminence that now so successfully challenges the dominance of the United States. Galbraith notes that taxes must be raised because investment, productivity, and economic growth are consistent or can be made consistent with higher taxes, but they cannot be reconciled with the high interest rates that are the alternative. He notes that the new federalism exacerbates the flaw in the American fiscal system of unequal sources of revenue. The federal government with its access to diverse tax sources and the tendency of its revenue sources to keep abreast of inflation is the best-financed unit of the three levels of government: federal, state, and local. The new federalism shifts public costs away from personal and corporate income tax bases to the more regressive sales and property tax bases of states and localities. The most important portent for the future is the lasting consequences of these policies. The removal of resources and governmental intervention for combating racism severely lessens the opportunities of the black disadvantaged in this country.

The problem, as I have tried to explain, is a political problem. Politics is the management of the conflict between groups warring over scarce resources, power, and status. If we are gathered here to assist the disadvantaged, we must consider the nature of the political struggle we intend to wage. This entails organization and political action. Racism has created two problems for African Americans: (1) unequal status based on the imputation of black inferiority; and (2) prior deprivation, which accrues educational deficits that need more time and opportunity to redress. Whether or not we at this conference are ready to tackle these problems remains to be seen. I shall make several recommendations, nevertheless.

Recommendations

The people at this conference and in every organization or institution concerned with public education in the United States must do the following.

- Work toward goals of excellent, high-quality education for every student, including the black poor.

- Lobby against and protest any school organization that permits the students to sink below national norms in reading and mathematics and demand its reorganization toward more effective routines.
- Lobby and press for access to technology for black and poor students.
- Assume the responsibility, in any professional position held, to help the black and the poor receive the services that he or she is responsible for delivering.
- Revise the history of the United States so that the true history of the black man is taught, approaching his contributions through the concept of a human, civil, social, and political rights struggle rather than race relations or the great man theory.
- Fight the intrusion on public education in the name of tuition tax credits and vouchers.

There is no easy way to resolve without struggle the problem of racism in a culture where it is vigorous and hostile. The lives of Charles Sumner, Thaddeus Stevens, Frederick Douglass, and W.E.B. DuBois affirm this. Their lives tell us that we either struggle toward the future or retreat into the past. In order not to repeat the errors of the First Jim Crow period we must understand what happened to us and know the consequences. This knowledge may give us choices to make for our future. We are making those choices here today at Wingspread.

Notes

1. Paul Francis Black, *A Historical Study of the Structures and Major Functions of the Pittsburgh Board of Public Education*. Ph.D. Dissertation, University of Pittsburgh, 1972, pp. 19–20.

2. W.E.B. DuBois, *Black Reconstruction in America* (New York: Russell & Russell, Inc., 1935), p. 226.

3. Ibid, p. 641.

4. Ibid, p. 665.

5. Ibid, p. 667.

6. Ibid, p. 665.

7. Richard Kluger, *Simple Justice* (New York: Vintage Books, A Division of Random House, 1977), pp. 61–62. See also John Hope Franklin, *From Slavery to Freedom* (New York: Alfred A. Knopf, 1947), pp. 324–43.

8. Kluger, *Simple Justice*, p. 50.

9. Rayford W. Logan, *The Betrayal of the Negro* (London: Collier-MacMillan Lt.), pp. 119–21.

10. Kluger, *op. cit.*, p. 80.

11. Derrick Bell, *Shades of Brown* (New York: Teachers College Press, Columbia University, 1980). See also Richard Kluger, *Simple Justice*, p. 534.

12. Kluger, *Simple Justice*, p. 540.

13. DuBois, *Black Reconstruction*, p. 283.

14. Thomas Sowell, *Black Education: Myths and Tragedies* (David McKay Co., 1972, pp. 283–86). See also Mary Gibson Hundley, *The Dunbar Story: 1870–1955* (Vantage Press, 1965).

15. James Coleman et al., *Equality of Educational Opportunity* (Washington, D.C.: U.S. Department of Health, Education and Welfare, Office of Education. U.S. Government Printing Office, 1966). See also Kenneth B. Clark, *The Dark Ghetto* (New York: Harper & Row, 1965), pp. 111–53; Patricia Cayo Sexton, *Education and Income* (New York: The Viking Press, 1961); *The Journal of Afro-American Issues: Testing, Measurements and Afro-Americans*, III, 1 (Winter, 1975); and Thomas F. Pettigrew, *A Profile of the Negro American* (New York: D. Van Nostrand Co., Inc., 1964), Chapter 4, pp. 100–135.

16. Arthur R. Jensen, "How Much Can We Boost I.Q. and Scholastic Achievement?" *Harvard Educational Review*, 39 (Winter, 1969), pp. 1–123.

17. Frank Reissman, *The Culturally Deprived Child* (New York: Harper & Row, 1962). See also Charles A. Valentine, *Culture and Poverty* (University of Chicago Press, 1968); Martin Deutsch, "Facilitating Development in the Preschool Child: Social and Psychological Perspectives," in *The Disadvantaged Child: Studies of the Social Environment and the Learning Process*, edited by Martin Deutsch and associates (New York: Basic Books, 1967), pp. 61–62.

18. Daniel Patrick Moynihan, *The Negro Family: The Case for National Action* (U.S. Government Printing Office, 1965). See also Edward C. Banfield, *The Unheavenly City* (Boston: Little, Brown and Co., 1970) and Stephen S. Baratz and Joan C. Baratz, "Early Childhood Intervention: The Social Science Base of Institutional Racism," in *As The Twig Is Bent*, edited by Robert H. Anderson and Harold G. Shane (Boston: Houghton Mifflin Co., 1971, pp. 34–52).

19. Ronald R. Edmonds, "Some Schools Work and More Can," *Social Policy* (March/April, 1979), pp. 28–32. See also Barbara A. Sizemore, "Push Politics and the Education of America's Youth," *Phi Delta Kappan* (January, 1979), pp. 364–69; Donald H. Smith, "The Black Revolution and Education," in *Black Self-Concept*, edited by James A. Banks and Jean D. Grambs (McGraw Hill Book Company, 1971), pp. 46–52; Henry M. Levin, "What Difference Do Schools Make?" *Saturday Review* (January 20, 1968), pp. 57–58; Baratz and Baratz, "Early Childhood Intervention"; John I. Goodlad, "Can Our Schools Get Better?" *Phi Delta Kappan* (January, 1979), pp. 342–46.

20. John U. Ogbu, *The Next Generation* (New York: Academic Press, 1974). See also Sara Lawrence Lightfoot and Jean V. Carew, *Beyond Bias* (Cambridge, Mass: Harvard University Press, 1979).

21. Barbara A. Sizemore, "Educational Research on Desegregation: Significance for the Black Community," *The Journal of Negro Education*, XLVII, 1 (Winter, 1978), pp. 59–68. See also Nancy L. Arnez, "Implementation of Desegregation as a Discriminatory Process/Genocidal Alternative," *The Journal of Negro Education*, Special Issue on Desegregation, XLVII, 1 (Winter, 1978), pp. 28–45; Charles V. Willie, *The Sociology of Urban Education* (Lexington, Massachusetts: Lexington Books, D.C. Heath and Co., 1978), pp. 59–76.

22. "Desegregation in the 1970's: A Candid Discussion," *The Journal of Negro Education,* XLVII, 1 (Winter, 1978). Robert G. Newby, "Desegregation: Its Inequities and Paradoxes: Toward an Equitable and Just Educational Policy for Afro-Americans," unpublished manuscript, Wayne State University, Detroit, Michigan, April, 1979. *Just Schools,* a Special Report Commemorating the 25th Anniversary of the Brown Decision, *Southern Exposure,* VII (Summer, 1979). Everett Abney, *A Survey of Black Public School Principals Employed in Florida During the 1964–65 School Term* (Coral Gables, Florida, University of Miami, 1976). Nancy H. St. John, *School Desegregation: Outcomes for Children* (New York: John Wiley & Sons, 1975). Jacquelyne J. Jackson and Larry C. Harris, "You May Be Normal When You Come Here, but You Won't Be Normal When You Leave, or Herman, the Pushout," *The Black Scholar,* VIII (April, 1977), 2–11. Ira Simmons, "The Whitening of Central," *The Louisville Times,* December 21, 1976.

23. Barbara A. Sizemore, *The Ruptured Diamond: The Politics of the Decentralization of the District of Columbia Public Schools* (Washington, D.C.: University Press of America, 1981), pp. 16–17, 43–49. See also *Equal Educational Opportunity,* Part 13, Quality and Control of Urban Schools, Hearings before the Select Committee on Equal Educational Opportunity, U.S. Senate, 92nd Congress, First Session (Washington, D.C.: U.S. Government Printing Office, July 27–29, August 5, 1971), pp. 5844–5912; Marilyn Gittell, "Community Control of Education," in *The Politics of Education,* edited by Marilyn Gittell and Alan G. Hevesi (New York: Praeger Publishers, 1967), pp. 363–77; Marilyn Gittell, *Participants and Participation* (New York: Praeger Publishers, 1967); Henry M. Levin, editor, *Community Control of Schools* (Washington, D.C.: The Brookings Institute, 1970); George R. LaNoue and Bruce L.R. Smith, *The Politics of Decentralization* (Lexington, Massachusetts: D.C. Heath and Co., 1973); Naomi Levine, Ocean Hill–Brownsville: *A Case History of Schools in Crisis* (New York: Popular Library Paperback, 1967); Arthur D. Little, Inc., *Urban Education: Eight Experiments in Community Control,* Report to the Office of Economic Opportunity (Washington, D.C.: U.S. Government Printing Office, October 13, 1969); Preston Wilcox, "The Thrust toward Community Control of the Schools in the Black Communities," in *Racial Crisis in American Education,* edited by Robert L. Green (Chicago: Follett Educational Corporation, 1969), pp. 299–318; James G. Cibulka, "School Decentralization in Chicago," *Education and Urban Society,* VII (August, 1975), p. 422; Charles E. Wilson, "201 Steps toward Community Control," in *Schools against Children,* edited by Annette T. Rubinstein (New York: Monthly Review Press, 1970), pp. 211–27; Alan A. Altshuler, *Community Control* (Pegasus, 1970).

24. Barbara A. Sizemore, *The Ruptured Diamond,* p. 47. See also Reginald Stuart, "Community Boards Have Few Powers," *Race Relations Reporter,* II, 8 (May 3, 1971), pp. 10–11.

25. James S. Coleman, *Equality of Educational Opportunity.*

26. Ibid, p. 22.

27. *Report of the National Advisory Commission on Civil Disorders,* The New York Times, 1968. See also Bert E. Swanson, *The Struggle for Equality* (Hobbs, Doorman and Co., 1966); Barbara A. Sizemore, *The Ruptured Diamond,* Chapter 3, pp. 73–160.

28. Ronald R. Edmonds, "A Discussion of the Literature and Issues Related to Effective Schooling," unpublished manuscript, Harvard University, 1979, p. 7. See also Christopher Jencks et al., *Inequality: A Reassessment of the Effect of Family and Schooling in America* (New York: Basic Books, 1972). Ivan Illich, *Deschooling Society* (New York: Harper & Row, 1970), p. 4.

29. Jonathan Kozol, *Death at an Early Age: The Destruction of the Hearts and Minds of Negro Children in the Boston Public Schools* (Boston: Houghton Mifflin, 1967); John Holt, *The Underachieving School* (Pitman, 1969); Charles Silberman, *Crisis in the Classroom* (New York: Random House, 1970); Diana T. Slaughter, "Alienation of Afro-American Children," in *Cultural Pluralism,* edited by Edgar G. Epps (Berkeley, California: McCutchan Publishing Corp., 1974), pp. 144–169; James Herndon, *The Way It 'Spozed To Be* (New York: Bantam Books, 1965); Herbert R. Kohl, *Thirty-Six Children* (New York: New American Library/World, 1967); Bel Kaufman, *Up the Down Staircase* (Englewood Cliffs, New Jersey: Prentice-Hall Inc., 1964).

30. David Rogers, *110 Livingston Street: Politics and Bureaucracy in the New York City Schools* (New York: Random House, 1968), pp. 169, 192, 197, 215, 273, 284–85, 331. See also Samuel Bowles and Henry M. Levin, "The Determinants of Scholastic Achievement: An Appraisal of Some Recent Evidence," *The Journal of Human Resources,* 3 (1968), pp. 3–24; Samuel Bowles and Herbert Gintis, *Schooling in Capitalist America* (New York: Basic Books, 1976).

31. George Weber, "Inner City Children Can Be Taught to Read: Four Successful Schools," Occasional Paper No. 18 (Washington, D.C.: Council for Basic Education, 1971).

32. Wilber B. Brookover and Lawrence W. Lezotte, "Changes in Student Achievement," a study from a project carried out at the College of Urban Development, Michigan State University, Department of Education, Unpublished paper, 1977, pp. 57–58.

33. Ibid, p. 60. See also Lawrence W. Lezotte and Joseph Passalacqua, "Individual School Buildings: Accounting for Differences in Measured Pupil Performance," *Urban Educator* (October, 1978), pp. 283–93.

34. Brookover and Lezotte, *Changes,* pp. 79–83.

35. William A. Firestone and Robert E. Herriott, *Images of the School: An Exploration of the Social Organization of Elementary, Junior High and High Schools* (Philadelphia: Field Studies, Research for Better Schools, Inc., 1980).

36. Mary Haywood Metz, *Classrooms and Corridors* (Berkeley, California: University of California Press, 1978), p. 18.

37. Ibid.

38. Barbara A. Sizemore, "Discipline and Learning: A Paradox?" *The Review of Education,* 7, 1 (Winter, 1981), pp. 68–70.

39. Edmonds, "Some Schools Work," pp. 28–29. See also State of New York, Office of Educational Performance Review, "School Factors Influencing Reading Achievement: A Case Study of Two Inner City Schools," March, 1974.

40. Edmonds, "Some Schools Work," p. 32.

41. Black, *Historical Study,* p. 204.

42. Pittsburgh School Board, Bureau of Statistics, Pittsburgh, Pennsylvania.

Response by Alex C. Sherriffs

Our topic is "The Connection between Postsecondary Programs for the Disadvantaged and Elementary and Secondary Schools." Matters relating to this subject have been the focus of much of my professional life for the past 15 years.

Dr. Sizemore has given us a thorough and sensitive picture of the history of blacks and black education in the United States. She has presented significant information on the important area of research on effective schooling. She has painted a picture of current political forces and practices, and she has given us her recommendations. I compliment Dr. Sizemore—her paper stands on its own.

I wish to add some observations based on my California experience. I will attempt to share thoughts on (1) affirmative action and (2) the condition of the public schools and the preparation of school personnel. In each case I will emphasize the relationship between K-12 and higher education.

Let's start on a high note: Public higher education and public elementary and secondary schools in California and elsewhere are at last finding one another and are doing more creative things regarding the disadvantaged, goals and standards, and teacher preparation.

But let me try for a bit of perspective.

Psychologists have determined that creativity is generally greatest when a person has at least one foot on solid ground. With a certain basic security, a human being can then engage in original and flexible thought or action, without survival fears bringing on rigidity or narrowing one's efforts. For most of us in education in California today the ground is moving under both of our feet. We face legislative intervention on all fronts and from all levels as never before, and direction of our internal affairs by the executive branch as never before, in fact or in fantasy. We endure declining enrollments, not only that predictable from the birth dearth of yesteryear but also from reasons that often escape us. Our budgets are slashed several times a year. And with ever greater determination the professoriate within the academy demands layoff by seniority—not by merit, ethnicity, or other variables—and the halting steps that we have taken in affirmative action leave footprints potentially ever less permanent. Our anxieties are increased, too, as we are pushed to extend the role in higher education of preparation for the world of work, for in most cases what we in higher education can best offer is a true education for those who will work or are working. The human being differs from other animals in that each generation can stand on the shoulders of those who went before. Horizons can be deeper and broader. A new generation can start with greater knowledge of the history, the environment, the ideas, the mistakes, and the successes of the past. It is our responsibility to see that this continues to be so.

That we make progress in student affirmative action or in "improving access to higher education" is all the more remarkable considering the need for creativity in so doing—along with the forces that work against any creativity at all.

We have been able to advance a number of educational opportunity programs at the 19 institutions with which I work. These programs have been developed with care and affection and have involved as many individuals and constituencies as we could find excuses to bring in—trustees, faculty, students, and administrators in our higher education segment; school board members, administrators, teachers, and counselors from elementary and secondary education. The internal education and sensitization process is a necessary first step. A good deal of this has been accomplished, I believe, and the momentum is with us if we can take advantage of it. The central office has assigned staff specifically to these efforts, individual institutions have done the same, and it is because we are working steadily on affirmative action that I can report to you that we have had successes and have gained some rather clear ideas about where we want and need to go, what we want and need to do in outreach, retention, and in making the values of affirmative action a part of the ongoing values of faculty and administrators.

For the California State University the Educational Opportunity Program, for those disadvantaged with potential but unable to meet traditional admissions requirements, has from its beginning provided major assistance in admitting minority and disadvantaged students and in offering important and necessary support services to those enrolled. An average of 3,500 new disadvantaged students have enrolled each year since 1969. Currently there are approximately 17,000 students in EOPs—approximately 30 percent of the California State University's minority population.

It is obvious that at the time the EOP was established our society was grossly ignoring its values for equal opportunity for all. This was as apparent in education as anywhere else. Along with the civil rights movement came heavy pressure on educational institutions to shape up. It was in this context that the EOP was established. In the beginning, of necessity it had to depend on untrained people, there was inadequate support for campus programs and for recruiting, and there was not a sufficient number of minority students graduating from high schools, either eligible for college admission or otherwise. At the time the emphasis almost had to be on exceptional admissions and remedial efforts. A sort of self-segregation resulted: students clung together on campuses, and programs were divided in part as home bases.

We also have a two-year-old, two million dollar student affirmative action program intended to produce a larger pool of high school graduates able to meet traditional entrance requirements. Unprecedented steps have been taken to help all university personnel to understand students who come from backgrounds different from their own. The influence of the forces represented by the civil rights movement was felt in K-12 as well as in higher education. In California more blacks and Mexican Americans are graduating from high school today.

One cannot be totally immersed in all this without developing some personal convictions as to what is crucial if we are in fact to provide equal opportunity for a quality education. This must mean more than equal opportunity for admittance; it must also mean a somewhat equal likelihood for success once enrolled in college.

The following considerations are critical at this time in history.

1. Role models are important, even necessary, and from the earliest years—to inspire, encourage, or even make it possible for the youth of underrepresented ethnic minorities to go forward in education. I speak here of members of the ethnic communities who would be inspirational to youth. Too few are invited, or see a responsibility for going regularly, to the schools where the young are to be found. Other important role models include educators of the same ethnic background who hold positions in colleges and universities, so that the young potential dropout would be encouraged to go on and stay on, and well-prepared minority teachers in the schools to help motivate students to aspire to higher achievement.

2. We should be deeply concerned that there are people significant to the young black and Hispanic—for example, counselors and teachers and professors—who, with or without prejudice, still have expectations that are different for blacks and browns than for whites and Orientals.

All too many youngsters are "advised" into noncollege preparatory programs simply on the basis of their complexion rather than on the basis of their intellectual potential. I do not see this as solely a responsibility of K-12. We in higher education produce the teachers and the counselors—and, for that matter, the administrators who provide leadership to those teachers and counselors. Many of them return to our classrooms throughout their careers, and we perhaps do not take advantage of their presence. The same problems exist at community colleges.

3. The second concern leads to a third—namely, that most solutions to what are very real problems require breaking down the barriers between various systems of higher education and between higher education and elementary and secondary schools. Many programs that seem without possibility for cure within any one perspective are viewed more optimistically

when we look together and observe together across education system lines.

4. Outreach needs to be defined these days in terms of students who are able to go on in education and who have potential motivation to do so. In California our attention was too limited to interest in unprepared students for whom side and back doors were necessarily opened during the sixties and early seventies. (As a matter of fact 15 percent of freshmen and sophomores at my institution even now enter as exceptions.) Especially is this an important matter to think through when one considers the academic mortality rate of those who enter unprepared and most of whom drop out in frustration soon afterward.

An institution that takes upon itself the responsibility to admit a class of students must also assume the responsibility to make it possible for these students to achieve and to survive. I refer, of course, to learning centers, tutoring, remedial reading and writing efforts, and a general ambience of welcome and understanding.

5. For our women students from kindergarten through higher education (they outnumber the men) there should be encouragement to enter courses and majors and to have aspirations heretofore reserved to males—for example, business, medicine, and engineering.

Finally, I would like to make an inflammatory observation. As I observe in school district after school district the absence at this late date of data on ethnic groups, so that we cannot know whether things are improving or not improving, and why and how—when I observe the demand for bilingual teachers and the inability of districts to find individuals who are motivated enough to become bilingual even in order to get a job—and when I observe the persistence of the pictures in people's heads about the human potential of others with skins different from their own, I sometimes come close to believing that much of what we have accomplished in these past years is a shift from active bigotry to passive indifference. In the community of Los Angeles, for example, this year 77.6 percent of the school population will be minority. (47.5 percent are Hispanic, 22.4 percent white, 22.2 percent black, 7.5 percent Asian, and .4 percent Indian and native Alaskan.) Who can conceivably assume that the community can remain viable without educating a significant percentage of its "minority" population, now a huge majority, for economic self-sufficiency, vision, and leadership? Those who do so must believe in an intolerable something that Kipling referred to as "the white man's burden." That is totally unacceptable.

Now to shift emphasis to the public schools and the role of higher education in preparing their teachers, counselors, and administrators. Today we find a public quite disillusioned with its public schools. The matter is extremely complex, and only pieces of it are within the purview of higher education. However, we do have significant responsibility for understanding what is involved, and for doing our very best in the areas in which we do have influence.

When visiting a statewide school association a few months ago I made the following comments.

Looking at it [the situation] in California, neither from the vantage point of a School of Education nor from that within a school district, one gets certain impressions. These include:

The preparation of teachers these days must include recognition of the many new responsibilities mandated to the schools, including nutrition, transportation, cultural differences, relations between ethnic groups, sex education, drug abuse, violence, and on and on.

But the typical college student who is to become a high school teacher doesn't identify himself or herself until the latter part of the junior year—or later still; neither the School of Education nor the student know one another, and it is a little late to advise on academic courses to prepare the candidate for much of the challenge ahead. In fact, there is too often little awareness of what is ahead. For the elementary teacher an earlier relationship develops. We had best consider the relationships of specific college preparation to the effective teaching of the very young.

The typical student preparing to become a teacher is still expecting pupils with starry eyes waiting to drink in knowledge about human beings, their history, their environment, their ideas, and the ways they have tried to live together. As teachers in the field tell us—there are too few with starry eyes. "Why should I?", "Try to make me", and minimal effort are more typical. The new teacher is in for shock for which there should have been preparation. Today it may well be that individuals with different motivations and personalities will make better teachers than was true in the past.

The teacher was once a part of the extended family; today that is much less the case. However, the teacher is still one of the truly vital factors in preparing the young for participation in a free society. Ironically, teachers now have too little respect and love from the public and are paid near the bottom of the professional scale. More tragic—for a make-or-break profession for our society—the bottom quartile of grades and ability are most often represented by those who choose to become teachers.

And lawmakers legislate countless "do's and don'ts" for teacher preparation, usually understanding only a part of the picture before passing their bills. In California they are about to do a major overhaul of teacher education law, and I believe they know even less than I do.

There is a tremendous need for adequacy in basic skills in students graduating from our high schools. But we cannot turn out teachers for mathematics instruction. Why? Because a person prepared to be a mathematics teacher can make several times the salary in industry, and can find employment there at once.

We emphasize academic depth by requiring a subject area major. We shy away from requiring professional courses in education thinking of them as "Blue Chalk 1A." Then the laws of California and the credentialing body work it out so that people who have majored in one area may teach another special area in the school program, and may be equipped neither for the substance of the area in question nor for how to present that subject matter so that learning will take place.

I was hoping that my listeners would say, "Oh, no, you are being too pessimistic." But instead they said, "You really have the picture."

Perhaps our greatest challenge is in teaching those who will become teachers. These are the people who will make or break our dreams in many areas. We in the California State University provide 40 percent of those who will teach in California. The public schools are failing. And yet, "while Rome burns," the general faculty on our campuses sit by and ridicule their second-class-citizen relatives, the faculties of the Schools of Education. If most of teacher preparation is to be done in departments other than education, then these departments are going to have to know more about the students in their classes and give them some attention as teachers in preparation. And especially they should understand the seriousness of what they are doing when they advise students against education as a career. They do this and they do it most forcefully with the most able students.

Somehow we have to make teaching and education respectable once again. The most idealistic and the most able should be attracted to the field. The inspiration and the constructive human motivation of the Peace Corps are quite appropriate for work in our public schools. But too few of us provide inspiration, and society will pay little for the services of those with teaching careers.

When a leading community such as Los Angeles, with a dozen university campuses within its boundaries, cannot produce 200 bilingual teachers or 25 mathematics teachers in a year—it is time to stop and think things through!

Editor's note:

During the discussion of the Sizemore paper and Sherriffs' response, a consensus emerged among the participants that, while Sizemore's work was impressive, its intentional focus on the black experience left a gap we would not want the final record of the proceedings to reflect—that is, we needed a Hispanic perspective on elementary and secondary education within the context of our deliberations. Alfredo de los Santos graciously yielded to the not-so-subtle pressures of colleagues to write such a paper to be included in this publication.

The Connection between Postsecondary Programs for Hispanics and Elementary and Secondary Schools

Alfredo G. de los Santos, Jr.

The institution that we refer to as education has had great difficulty in providing equal services to students whose mother language is other than English. At a time when the birthrate in the United States is decreasing and almost all enrollment projections for the public schools forecast a steady decline until the end of this decade, a wave of Hispanic youths is now entering the educational system or is about to do so. At a time when enrollments in institutions of higher education are declining, holding steady, or increasing at a very low rate, literally thousands of Hispanics have need of higher education.

While the title of this chapter limits its scope to the connection for Hispanics between the postsecondary and the elementary and secondary parts of our educational system, in effect it covers much more. Five separate but related sections include: (1) a brief description of the growth of the Hispanic population in the United States from 1970 to 1980 and some pertinent characteristics, (2) the use of Spanish by Hispanics and the effect on their participation in education and academic achievement, (3) Hispanics and their involvement in elementary and secondary education, (4) Hispanic access, attrition, and achievement in postsecondary education, and (5) the educational pipeline for Hispanics, which shows their leakage from the system.

Hispanic Population in the United States: Size and Characteristics

This section outlines basic information about the size and distribution of the Hispanic population in this country and some of this population's pertinent characteristics.

68

Size and distribution

In February 1981 the Bureau of the Census of the United States Department of Commerce announced that the number of Hispanics in this country in 1980 was 14,605,883 or 6.4 percent of the total population of 226,504,825. This compared with a 1970 count of 9,072,602 persons of Spanish origin, or 4.5 percent of the total population of 203,211,926. The increase of more than five million in the Hispanic population represents more than 60 percent growth in the 10-year period from 1970 to 1980. (U.S. Department of Commerce, Bureau of the Census, News CB81-32, Washington, D.C., February 1981.) Factors that may have accounted for this larger count included "better coverage of the population, improved question design, and an effective public relations campaign," but most significant for our purposes is the high percent of increase and the growth in absolute numbers.

A few months later, in July 1981, the Bureau announced the distribution of the Hispanic population, indicating that "more than three-fifths of the nation's 14.6 million Hispanics reside in California, Texas, and New York." California had a Hispanic population of 4,543,770, or 31.1 percent of the total United States Hispanic population; Texas, 2,985,643, or 20.4 percent of the total; and New York, 1,659,245, or 11.4 percent of the total. Table 1 shows the 10 states with the largest number of Hispanics, the Hispanic population in each state, the percentage Hispanics represent of the state's total, and the percentage of the total of Hispanics in the United States who reside in that state. (U.S. Department of Commerce, Bureau of the Census, News, CB81-118, Washington, D.C., July 1981.)

A significant majority, 8,785,717, lives in the five Southwestern states of

Table 1. 1980 Hispanic Population in the United States, 10 Top States

State	Rank	Hispanic Population	Hispanic Percentage of State Total	Percentage of U.S. Hispanic Population
California	1	4,543,770	19.2	31.1
Texas	2	2,985,643	21.0	20.4
New York	3	1,659,245	9.5	11.4
Florida	4	857,898	8.8	5.9
Illinois	5	635,525	5.6	4.4
New Jersey	6	491,867	6.7	3.4
New Mexico	7	476,089	36.6	3.3
Arizona	8	440,915	16.2	3.0
Colorado	9	339,300	11.7	2.3
Michigan	10	162,388	1.8	1.1

Arizona, California, Colorado, New Mexico, and Texas. This represents slightly more than 60 percent of the total United States Hispanic population.

In an earlier publication, the Bureau reported that persons of Mexican origin constitute approximately 60 percent of the total number of Hispanics; Puerto Ricans represent about 14.5 percent; Cubans, 6.6 percent; Central or South American, 7.0 percent; and other Spanish origin, 11.4 percent. (U.S. Department of Commerce, Bureau of the Census, 1980.)

Age of Hispanics

The Hispanic population as a group is more than eight years younger than the non-Hispanic population in the United States, as the median age of Hispanics is 22.0 years and that of non-Hispanics, 30.4. The median age of Puerto Ricans is 19.9, Mexicans 21.1, and Cubans 36.3. Another significant point is that more than 12.6 percent of the Hispanic population is under five years of age, compared to 6.9 for persons not of Spanish origin. (U.S. Department of Commerce, Bureau of the Census, 1980.)

Median income

The median income for Hispanics in 1978 was substantially lower than the income of non-Spanish persons: $5,893 for Hispanics compared with $6,864 for non-Hispanics. Approximately 21 percent of Hispanic men had incomes of $15,000 or more, compared with 36 percent of the non-Hispanic men who had income in this bracket. Yet Hispanic men earned an income significantly higher than Hispanic women; the average income for men was $8,380 and for women $3,788. (U.S. Department of Commerce, Bureau of the Census, 1980.)

Residence

The Hispanic population is more concentrated in metropolitan, urban areas than the non-Hispanic population, with the majority of Hispanics living in the central city. More than 85 percent of Hispanics live in metropolitan areas, compared with 65.8 percent of non-Hispanics. About 51 percent of Hispanics live in the central city, compared with 25.8 percent of persons not of Spanish origin. (U.S. Department of Commerce, Bureau of the Census, 1980.)

Hispanics, Language Usage, and Educational Participation

The Hispanic population in the United States retains its language more than any other ethnic group. San Juan Cafferty reports that "it is the Spanish-speaking who, as a people, have had the greatest retention of native language in the United States. In the case of the Mexican-American in the Southwest, retention of Spanish language and culture can be attributed to a proximity to Mexico and to the continuing stream of Mexican migrant workers, as well as to isolation and exclusion by the English-speaking society." (San Juan Cafferty, 1982, p. 111.)

The exclusion of the Spanish-speaking is especially noticeable in their participation in the educational system.

In 1975, approximately 13 percent of the population four years old and over of ethnic-origin groups in the United States lived in households where the language spoken was other than English. Of the Spanish-origin population, however, a whopping 85 percent lived in households where the household language spoken was Spanish and 41 percent usually spoke Spanish (see Figure 1).

The relationship between language usage and enrollment in the educational system is shown in Figure 2. Among the Hispanic population who were 14 to 18 years old, only 79 percent of those who lived in a household where a language other than English was spoken and who spoke a language other than English were enrolled, compared with 91 percent of those in the same age group who lived in households where English was the household language and who themselves spoke English. It is interesting to note that a slightly higher percentage—93 percent—of those who lived in a household where a language other than English was spoken but who usually spoke English were enrolled. Are these persons bilingual?

The relationship between language among Hispanics and their participation—or, rather, their nonparticipation—in the educational system is seen in Figure 3.

Figure 3 shows that while approximately 10 percent of the total population between the ages of 14 and 25 years of age—prime ages for students being enrolled in high school and college—had not completed four years of high school and were not enrolled during the 1974-75 school year, the percentage of Hispanics in the same age group was more than double that figure—approximately 24 percent.

Fifteen percent of those who had claimed Spanish origin and who lived in households where only English was spoken had dropped out of high school, compared with 10 percent for the total. What is most significant is that a very large percentage—45 percent—of those persons who were between 14 and 25 years of age who claimed Spanish origin and who lived in households where Spanish was usually spoken and who themselves spoke Spanish had completed fewer than four years of high school and were not enrolled in school in the 1974-75 academic year. In effect, almost half of Hispanics in this age group who spoke Spanish and who lived in homes where Spanish was usually spoken had dropped out of high school without graduating.

Figure 1. Language Usage

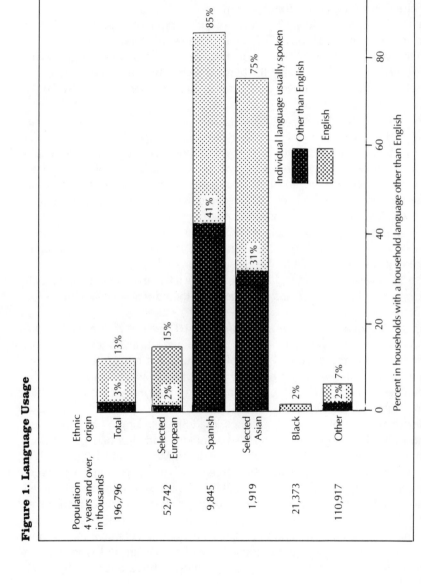

Source: National Center for Education Statistics, *The Condition of Education, 1977 edition, Statistical Report,* edited by M. A. Golladay, Vol. 3, Part 1 (Washington, D.C.: 1977), p. 9.

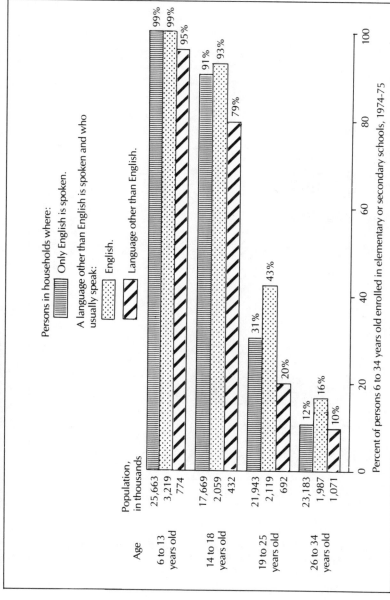

Source: National Center for Education Statistics, *The Condition of Education, 1977 edition, Statistical Report,* edited by M. A. Golladay, Vol. 3, Part 1 (Washington, D.C.: 1977), p. 94.

Figure 3. High School Dropouts, 14 to 25 Years Old by Language Characteristics

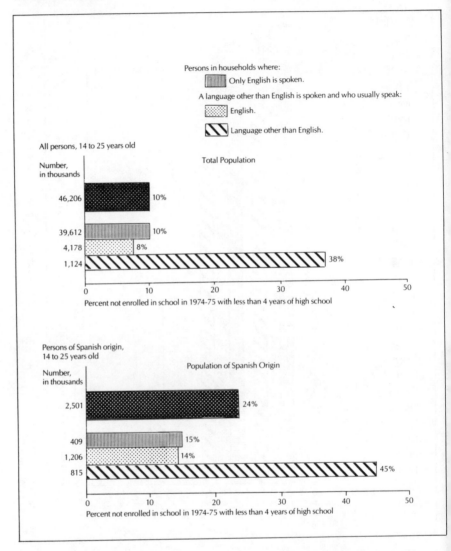

Source: National Center for Education Statistics, *The Condition of Education, 1977 edition, Statistical Report,* edited by M. A. Golladay, Vol. 3, Part 1 (Washington, D.C.: 1977), p. 98.

More recent studies of language minority students in younger age groups have shown that language is a very significant predictor of achievement in relationship to other related factors. A study of a large sample of children ($N = 408$) from seven ethnolinguistic groups concluded that proficiency in English was the most significant predictor of academic achievement relative to other factors, including cognitive style, cognitive development, and so forth (DeAvila 1981).

Another study (DeAvila 1980), which related ethnic background, socioeconomic status, language proficiency, and achievement in reading and mathematics, based on data from the California Assessment Program ($N = 12,000$), found that: (1) there were, as expected, significant differences in achievement; (2) controlling for socioeconomic background virtually eliminated all the differences between black and Anglo children and only slightly reduced, but did not eliminate, the differences with Hispanics; and (3) controlling for both language and socioeconomic status for Hispanics eliminated the differences.

To summarize, Hispanics, more than any other ethnic group, retain the use of their native language, and this usage (and the corollary lack of proficiency in the use of English) has a negative effect on their participation in the educational system and on academic achievement.

While some argue that "there is decreasing incidence of native language retention among Hispanics," (San Juan Cafferty, 1982, p. 103) recent studies indicate that large numbers of children of school age have limited proficiency in English. *The Children's English and Services Study* by the National Clearinghouse for Bilingual Education revealed that an estimated 2.4 million children with limited English-language proficiency, between the ages of 5 and 14 years, were living in the United States in 1978. More children in the 5-14 age group who lived in households where Spanish is spoken were limited in English proficiency than children of the same age living in households where other non-English languages were spoken. A total of 1.7 million children of Spanish-language background aged 5-14 had limited proficiency in English; this represents 73 percent of the total number of children in this age group living in households where Spanish is usually spoken.

Hispanics and the elementary and secondary educational system

The participation of Hispanics in the elementary and secondary educational system has been well documented. (See Carter and Segura, *Mexican Americans in School: A Decade of Change*, 1979; National Center for Education Statistics, *The Condition of Education for Hispanic Americans*, 1980; Durán, *Hispanics' Educational Attainment and Prediction of College*

Achievement, 1982.) Some of the important findings related to their achievement, the factors that interfere with the students' school work, are reported here.

Hispanic students (9-, 13-, and 17-year-olds) scored lower at a statistically significant level in 1971-75 than did non-Hispanic students of the same age in five areas: social studies, science, mathematics, career and occupational development, and reading. In fact, it seems as if the older the Hispanic students were, the greater the difference in four areas—social studies, science, mathematics, and reading (see Table 2).

Table 2. Achievement in Five Subject-Matter Areas for Hispanic and White Students 9-, 13-, and 17-Year-Olds, 1971-75

Subject Matter and Ethnic Group	Percentage Point Difference[1] from the National Average for:		
	9-year-olds	13-year-olds	17-year-olds
Social studies			
Hispanic	−10.59	−10.05	−13.12
White, non-Hispanic.	2.73	2.07	2.39
Science			
Hispanic	−9.53	−11.55	−11.08
White, non-Hispanic.	3.12	3.49	2.13
Mathematics			
Hispanic	−7.77	−11.71	−14.36
White, non-Hispanic.	2.76	3.74	3.63
Career and occupational development			
Hispanic	−14.08	−12.44	−7.65
White, non-Hispanic.	3.23	3.50	2.19
Reading			
Hispanic	−10.77	−11.25	−11.42
White, non-Hispanic.	2.54	2.73	2.78

1. All of the differences from the national norm in this table are statistically significant at the 0.05 level.

Source: National Center for Education Statistics, *The Condition of Education for Hispanic Americans,* compiled by G. H. Brown, S. T. Hill, N. Rosen, and M. A. Olivas (Washington, D.C.: National Center for Education Statistics, 1980), p. 222.

Five years later, the situation remained the same. A 1980 survey sponsored by the National Center for Education Statistics (1982) found that Hispanic students "have lower average scores on math, reading, and vocabulary tests than non-Hispanic whites." As shown in Table 3, the mean score of 11.6 in mathematics for non-Hispanic white seniors was more

Table 3. Mean Scores on Mathematics, Reading, and Vocabulary, by Population Subgroup, Spring 1980

Subgroup	Mathematics			Reading			Vocabulary		
	Sample size[1]	Mean score	Standard deviation	Sample size[1]	Mean score	Standard deviation	Sample size[1]	Mean score	Standard deviation
Sophomores									
Mexican-American. . . .	1,864	7.5	3.5	1,865	2.7	1.7	1,862	2.9	1.6
Cuban	259	8.7	4.3	248	3.5	2.1	254	3.4	2.1
Puerto Rican . . .	313	7.1	3.2	311	2.7	1.8	316	3.0	1.6
Other Latin American .	659	8.0	3.4	660	3.0	1.8	659	3.2	1.8
Non-Hispanic black . .	868	6.7	3.2	873	2.5	1.7	872	2.7	1.6
Non-Hispanic white . .	930	10.3	3.8	931	3.9	2.0	933	4.1	1.9
Seniors									
Mexican American. . . .	1,621	8.4	4.0	1,632	3.3	1.9	1,628	3.5	1.8
Cuban	286	10.1	4.3	292	3.9	2.1	292	4.2	1.9
Puerto Rican . . .	257	8.0	4.6	262	3.3	2.0	265	3.5	1.9
Other Latin American .	557	8.3	3.9	565	3.3	1.9	567	3.6	1.9
Non-Hispanic black . .	854	7.7	3.8	854	3.2	2.0	856	3.2	1.8
Non-Hispanic white . .	893	11.6	4.0	901	4.9	2.0	898	4.8	1.9

1. For comparison purposes and to reduce computation costs, simple random subsamples of 1,000 non-Hispanic whites and 1,000 non-Hispanic blacks were selected for the analysis. The sample sizes reported in the table reflect the actual number of students who provided data for the analysis.

Source: National Center for Education Statistics, *Bulletin,* NCES 82-228b, "Hispanic Students in American High Schools: Background Characteristics and Achievement" (Washington, D.C.: National Center for Education Statistics, July 1982), p. 7.

than three points higher than the mean scores for Mexican American and Puerto Rican seniors. In reading, the 3.3 mean score for Mexican American and Puerto Rican seniors was 1.6 points lower than the 3.9 mean score for non-Hispanic white seniors. Non-Hispanic white seniors had a mean score in vocabulary of 4.8, which was 1.3 points higher than the 3.5 mean score for Mexican American and Puerto Rican seniors.

Factors cited by both Hispanic and non-Hispanic white seniors in 1972 as interfering with their school work indicate some that are common and some that seem to affect Hispanic students more. Durán (1982), elaborating on data included in *The Condition of Education for Hispanic Americans*, noted that "both Hispanic and White non-Hispanic senior high school students agreed to more or less the same extent that the following factors inhibited school work: "School doesn't offer the courses I want to take;" "Don't feel part of the school;" "Poor study habits;" "Find it hard to adjust to school routine;" and "My job takes too much time," (see Table 4).

However, as shown in Figure 4, four factors for which the difference was greatest between the Hispanic seniors and the non-Hispanic white seniors

Table 4. Factors cited by Hispanic and White High School Seniors as Interfering with Their School Work, 1972

Factors	Percentage[1] Who Answered "Somewhat" or "a Great Deal"	
	Hispanic	White, non-Hispanic
Worry over money problems (repayment of loan, support of dependents, family income, etc.)	45.5	27.4
Family obligations (other than money problems)	39.3	23.6
Lack of a good place to study at home	36.7	22.1
Parents aren't interested in my education	33.7	19.4
Courses are too hard	49.9	41.0
Teachers don't help me enough	54.1	47.3
My own ill health	16.7	10.3
Transportation to school is difficult	15.9	9.6
School doesn't offer the courses I want to take	45.5	50.3
Don't feel part of the school	39.5	35.5
Poor teaching	46.4	50.3
Poor study habits	59.7	57.2
Find it hard to adjust to school routine	24.3	22.9
My job takes too much time	19.1	19.3

1. Students could make multiple responses. Factors are listed in descending order of the size of difference between Hispanics and white, non-Hispanics.

Source: National Center for Education Statistics, *The Condition of Education for Hispanic Americans,* compiled by G. H. Brown, S. T. Hill, N. Rosen, and M. A. Olivas (Washington, D.C.: 1980), p. 70.

Figure 4. Factors Interfering with School Work of High School Seniors

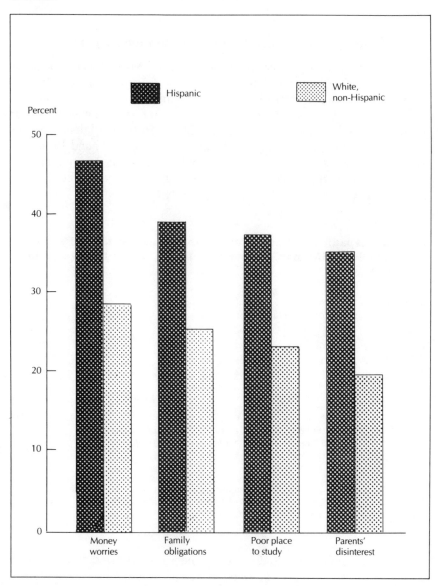

Source: National Center for Education Statistics. *The Condition of Education for Hispanic Americans.* Compiled and edited by G. H. Brown, S. T. Hill, N. Rosen, and M. A. Olivas (Washington, D.C.: 1980), p. 71.

all seem related to family and familial style: worry over money problems, family obligations, poor place to study, and disinterest on the part of parents.

The secondary-to-postsecondary connection for Hispanics

The connection between secondary education and postsecondary education invariably leads to the community college for the majority of those Hispanics who do graduate from high school. A study of access, attrition, and achievement of Hispanic students in public institutions of higher education showed that approximately 85 percent of all the Hispanic students enrolled in California institutions of higher education in 1976, 1977, and 1978 were enrolled in the community college, if only undergraduate enrollment is considered. If both graduate and undergraduate enrollment is considered, the percentage drops slightly to approximately 82 percent (see Table 5).

Table 5. Hispanic Headcount Enrollment Comparisons, Fall 1976 to Fall 1978, in California Community Colleges, Senior Colleges, and Universities

Undergraduate Enrollment Only	Community/Junior Colleges		Senior Colleges		Total
	Number	Percent	Number	Percent	Number
1976	108,880	85.50	18,470	14.50	127,350
1977	117,662	86.70	18,061	13.31	135,723
1978	109,638	84.17	20,625	15.83	130,263

Total Enrollment	Community/Junior Colleges		Senior Colleges		Total
	Number	Percent	Number	Percent	Number
1976	108,880	82.70	22,785	17.31	131,665
1977	117,662	84.14	22,180	15.86	139,842
1978	109,638	81.38	25,084	18.62	134,722

Source: De los Santos, A. G., Jr.; J. Montemayor; and E. Solis, Jr., Chicano Students in Institutions of Higher Education: Access, Attrition, and Achievement (Austin: University of Texas, College of Education, 1980), p. 42.

In Texas, if only undergraduate enrollment is considered approximately 60 percent of all Hispanics enrolled in public institutions of higher education were enrolled in community colleges (see Table 6). If the total enrollment is considered, then approximately 55 percent were enrolled in community colleges (de los Santos 1980; see also Olivas, The Dilemma of Access, 1979).

Table 6. Hispanic Headcount Enrollment Comparisons, Fall 1976 to Fall 1978, in Texas Community/Junior Colleges, Senior Colleges, and Universities

Undergraduate Enrollment Only	Community/Junior Colleges		Senior Colleges		Total
	Number	Percent	Number	Percent	Number
1976	35,423	60.04	23,571	39.96	58,994
1977	36,872	59.48	25,113	40.51	61,985
1978	38,517	58.16	27,705	41.84	66,222

Total Enrollment	Community/Junior Colleges		Senior Colleges		Total
	Number	Percent	Number	Percent	Number
1976	35,423	55.86	27,991	44.15	63,414
1977	36,872	55.19	27,943	44.81	66,315
1978	38,517	54.04	32,746	45.95	71,263

Source: De los Santos, A. G., Jr.; J. Montemayor; and E. Solis, Jr., *Chicano Students in Institutions of Higher Education: Access, Attrition, and Achievement* (Austin: University of Texas, College of Education, 1980), p. 43.

Attrition

This same study reported that "at both the two-year and four-year institutions, Hispanics have significantly higher attrition rates and lower retention rates than do non-Hispanics." Some of the other findings of this study include:

- Both "native" and community college transfer Hispanics have higher attrition and lower retention rates than the average at the California State University and Colleges.
- Hispanic females have lower attrition rates and higher completion rates—as do female students of all ethnic groups—than their male counterparts in the California State University and Colleges.
- Attrition rates are higher in the Texas public community and junior colleges than in the senior institutions, which actually gain enrollment after the sophomore year.

Achievement

In terms of achievement, defined simply as degrees earned, the study reported that "the percentage of degrees earned by Hispanics at all levels is disproportionately lower than the percentage Hispanics represent of the total population" and "Hispanics earn a disproportionately higher number of associate degrees relative to all other degrees earned by them" (de los Santos, 1980, pp. 116-117).

In 1975-76 of the 42,527 degrees earned by Hispanics, almost half, or 20,065 were associate's degrees; 18,165, or slightly more than 42 percent, were bachelor's; less than 10 percent, or 4,033, were master's; and only 264 were doctoral degrees (see Table 7).

Table 7. Distribution of Degrees Earned Nationally in Public Institutions, 1975-76

| | | Hispanics | | | | | |
Level of Degree	Total Degrees	Male	% of total degrees	Female	% of total degrees	Total	% of total degrees
Associate's......	429,844	10,749	2.50	9,316	2.17	20,065	4.67
Bachelor's	634,197	9,513	1.50	8,652	1.36	18,165	2.86
Master's.........	205,228	2,018	0.98	2,015	0.98	4,033	1.96
Doctorate.......	21,618	194	0.90	70	0.32	264	1.22
Total.............	1,290,887	22,474	1.74	20,053	1.55	42,527	3.29

Source: De los Santos, A. G., Jr.; J. Montemayor; and E. Solis, Jr., *Chicano Students in Institutions of Higher Education: Access, Attrition, and Achievement* (Austin: University of Texas, College of Education, 1980), p. 95.

Table 8, taken from *The Condition of Education for Hispanic Americans,* shows that Hispanics earned 2 percent or less of all the bachelor's, master's, doctor's, and first professional degrees awarded in 1976-77. Hispanics earned approximately 4 percent of all associate's degrees awarded.

Educational Pipeline for Hispanics

The relative high attrition rate of Chicano and Puerto Ricans from the educational system and the relative few who do eventually earn degrees are shown in the figure in Chapter 7, "Minorities in Higher Education." Beginning with a cohort of 100 students, only 55 Chicanos and 55 Puerto Ricans will graduate from high school, compared with 83 white students and 72 blacks. Of the 100, only 22 Chicanos and 25 Puerto Ricans will enroll in an institution of higher education, compared with 38 whites and 29 blacks.

Only 7 Chicanos and 7 Puerto Ricans out of 100 will complete college, compared with 23 whites and 12 blacks. Only 4 Chicanos and 4 Puerto

Table 8. Degrees Earned by Hispanics on U.S. Mainland and in Puerto Rico/Territories, by Level of Degrees, 1976-77

Degrees Earned by Hispanics

Level of Degree	Aggregate U.S.[1] Total degrees (number)	U.S. Mainland[2] Number	Percent of degrees earned by all students on U.S. mainland	Puerto Rico/Territories Number	Percent of all degrees earned by Hispanics (aggregate U.S.)[1]
Associate degrees[3]					
Total......	24,092	20,834	4.1	3,258	13.5
Male ...	12,514	11,405	4.4	1,109	8.9
Female	11,578	9,429	3.8	2,149	18.6
Bachelor's					
Total......	26,963	18,663	2.0	8,300	30.8
Male ...	13,672	10,238	2.1	3,434	25.1
Female	13,291	8,425	2.0	4,866	36.6
Master's					
Total......	7,069	6,069	1.9	1,000	14.1
Male ...	3,665	3,266	2.0	399	10.9
Female	3,404	2,803	1.9	601	17.7
Doctor's					
Total......	534	522	1.6	12	2.2
Male ...	391	383	1.5	8	2.0
Female	143	139	1.7	4	2.8
First-professional					
Total......	1,478	1,076	1.7	402	27.2
Male ...	1,174	893	1.7	281	23.9
Female	304	183	1.5	121	39.8

1. Awarded by institutions of higher education in the 50 states, D.C., Puerto Rico, and territories in the school year 1976-1977.

2. Fifty states and District of Columbia.

3. Includes associate degrees and other formal awards for less than four years of work beyond high school.

Source: National Center for Education Statistics, The Condition of Education for Hispanic Americans, compiled by G. H. Brown, S. T. Hill, N. Rosen, and M. A. Olivas (Washington, D.C.: 1980, p. 164).

Ricans will enter graduate or professional school, compared with 14 whites and 8 blacks. Only 2 Chicanos and 2 Puerto Ricans out of 100 will complete graduate or professional school compared with 8 whites and 4 blacks (Astin 1982).

References

Astin, Alexander W., *Minorities in American Higher Education.* San Francisco: Jossey-Bass, 1982.

Carter, Thomas P., and Roberto D. Segura, *Mexican Americans in School: A Decade of Change.* New York: College Entrance Examination Board, 1979.

De Avila, Edward, et al., *The Language Minority Child: A Psychological, Linguistic and Educational Analysis.* Larkspur, California: De Avila, Duncan and associate, 1981.

De Avila, Edward, *Relative Language Proficiency Types: A comparison of Prevalence, Achievement Level and Socioeconomic Status.* Larkspur, California, Delta Square, Inc., 1980.

de los Santos, Alfredo G., Jr. Joaquin Mentemayor and Enrique Solis, *Chicano Students in Institutions of Higher Education: Access, Attrition and Achievement.* Austin: University of Texas, 1980.

Duran, Richard P., *Hispanics' Educational Attainment and Prediction of College Achievement: A Review of Selected Background Issues and Selected Research.* Princeton: Educational Testing Service, 1982.

National Center for Education Statistics. *The Condition of Education for Hispanic Americans.* Compiled and edited by G. H. Brown, N. L. Rosen, S. T. Hill, and M. A. Olivas. Washington, D.C.: 1980.

National Center for Education Statistics. *The Condition of Education: Statistical Report, 1978 edition.* Washington, D.C., 1978.

National Center for Education Statistics. *Bulletin,* NCES 82-228b. "Hispanic Students in American High Schools: Background Characteristics and Achievements." Washington, D.C., July 1982.

National Clearinghouse for Bilingual Education. *Children's English and Services Study: Language Minority Children with Limited English Proficiency in the United States.* By J. Michael O'Malley. Rosslyn, Virginia, 1981.

San Juan Cafferty, Pastora, "The Language Question: The Dilemma of Bilingual Education for Hispanics in America," in *Ethnic Relations in America* by the American Assembly. Englewood Cliffs, New Jersey; Prentice-Hall, 1982.

Olivas, Michael A., *The Dilemma of Access: Minorities in Two-Year Colleges.* Washington, D.C.: Institute for the Study of Educational Policy, 1979.

U.S. Department of Commerce. Bureau of the Census, *News,* CB 81-32. Washington, D.C., February 1981.

U.S. Department of Commerce. *News.* CB 81-118. Washington, D.C.: July 1981.

U.S. Department of Commerce. *Persons of Spanish Origin in the United States.* March, 1979. Population Characteristics Series p. 20, No. 354, Washington, D.C.: 1980.

New Populations, New Arrangements

Michael A. Olivas

Rereading *Barriers to Higher Education* is a decidedly frustrating exercise in déjà vu. The prescience shown by the 1970 authors is in many ways quite extraordinary, while the subsequent lack of progress—and in many cases, the pronounced reversals of progress—suggests their profound naivete about the extent of change possible without institutional reorientation. In my native New Mexico we burn zozobra (a figure called "Old Man Gloom") each year, in time-honored scapegoating fashion, in the hope that the pyre will rid Hispanos of the year's accumulation of grief and indignities. My paper is this session's zozobra, as I must offer up the facts and figures on the retreats from the hopes of 1970 and challenge several widely held assumptions about "increased" access. Most notably, it is difficult to reconstruct the optimistic mood in which the 1970 conference was conducted, as many gains have been eroded and harsher economic conditions prevail.

Optimism is unwarranted because of a verifiable decline in minority access, because of a changed mood in larger communities concerning access, and because of continued intransigence on the part of institutions. While each of these phenomena is worthy of its own conference, I will limit myself to summarizing the first two concerns—documenting the decline and noting the changed mood—and will explain myself more fully in the critical charge I make of institutional intransigence. While these remarks will surely seem a jeremiad to the unconvinced, I insist that they represent the views of many colleagues who have, over the years, worked within the system to improve access for populations previously (and legally) excluded from higher education. In many cases, higher education as an institution has not deserved the loyalty it has received from my colleagues, who have placed extraordinary faith in higher education's fundamental fairness—only to find it unjustified.

Declines in Access

Because most majority Americans continue to view minority access solely as black admissions into white colleges, the complexity of minority inequities is often misunderstood. First, black admissions to white institutions have peaked, and since 1977 have leveled off (Morris 1979; Institute for the Study of Educational Policy 1980), severely undermining the apparent gains. Equally serious has been the decline of support for black colleges, whose existence is frequently (and wrongly) perceived as anachronistic in a society that views itself as more sympathetic than earlier U.S. societies, when segregation was given force of law. Black colleges are under more subtle attack in the form of the *Adams v. Califano*[1] litigation, leading to the "desegregation" of black institutions. While an analysis of the *Adams* case is beyond the scope of this paper, suffice it to say that the major impact of the litigation has been to call into question the survival of black colleges (Haynes 1978; Morris 1979): desegregation plans have been drafted, institutions have been merged (e.g., the University of Tennessee at Nashville merged with Tennessee State University), and legislation has been amended to incorporate *Adams* issues. Southern and Northern states have submitted *Adams* plans to the Office for Civil Rights and the courts for approval, and the Higher Education Act of 1965 recently reauthorized by Congress contains language requiring that federal programs comply with *Adams* mandates.[2]

Access for women has increased, to the extent that they constitute a majority of entering freshman students. Nonetheless, women take fewer advanced degrees (only 30 percent of doctorates in 1979-80) (Gilford and Snyder 1977) and hold fewer administrative positions in higher education (Astin 1977) than should be the case if sexism were not operating in the marketplace. In women's studies programs, whose existence provides one measure of academic progress, there has been phenomenal growth since 1967, when only two colleges reported such curricula (Wood 1981). However, more telling to my thesis, these programs appear to flourish and take root only when institutional behavior is modified to a significant extent to create a climate favorable to establishing the courses, hiring the faculty, and designing the curriculum.

Indian students continue to be overlooked and underserved. Even with questionable counts and self-identification (one Midwestern college increased its official count of Native American students from 11 to over 500 when non-Indians mischievously misidentified themselves as "native" Americans), Indian students constitute less than 1 percent of all full-time

---

1. 430 F. Supp. 118 (D.D.C. 1977).

2. Title III, Sec. 307 (2), for example, prohibits payments "for an activity that is inconsistent with a state plan for desegregation of higher education applicable to such institution."

undergraduates. In 1979-80 only 106 doctorates were awarded to Indians (of a total of 30,982 doctoral degrees), half in the field of education. As small as these numbers are, in many respects they may represent the peak of Indian degrees, as recent federal developments have seriously undermined long-term efforts to increase Indian access to higher education. First, because of the unique federal trust responsibilities to Indian people, cuts in the Bureau of Indian Affairs (BIA) and other federal budgets disproportionately affect Indians, who, in most cases, do not have complete sovereignty over their own governance. Both Indian set-aside programs and Indian participation in larger social programs are jeopardized, as the historical marginalization of Indian affairs has rendered tribes and Indian people exceptionally vulnerable, even in good times. Second, the delays and problems of the Tribally Controlled Community College Assistance Act have seriously affected the ability of these unique institutions to develop and serve Indian students (Olivas 1982).

Hispanic higher education has received increased attention in recent years (Lopez et al. 1976; Olivas and Hill 1980; Olivas 1981), although the area has not been sufficiently examined even by equity researchers or bilingual educators, for systemic and structural disadvantages facing Hispanic learners are so great at all levels of education and so intertwined with the politically powerless status of Hispanics that neither the nature nor the severity of the disadvantage is fully understood. As an example, from 1970 to 1978, Hispanic full-time students increased only from 2.1 percent of the total to 3.5 percent. These figures represent a peak enrollment period, as the percentage declined to 3.4 percent in 1980 (Olivas and Hill 1980, Table 3.09; and unpublished National Center for Educational Statistics data). Moreover, because Hispanic students do not have access to a network of historically Hispanic colleges (Olivas 1982b), they must rely on majority colleges. In fact, 21 mainland colleges enroll 43 percent of all mainland Hispanic students—an extraordinary concentration—a fact to which I will allude later.

Asian education is an extraordinary example of how statistical evidence and popular opinion can be marshalled to portray racial groups as advantaged, despite substantial evidence to the contrary. For instance, a recent popular study of minorities in higher education omitted mention of Asians, tacitly suggesting that Asian education did not merit such scrutiny.[3] Rather, this insidious viewpoint fails to acknowledge the recent history of racism against Asians that in no small part resulted in exclusionary immigration practices leading to an educated elite among Asians. Ironically, this statu-

---

3. The study's board had an Asian member, praised in the report for adding "a background to [board] deliberations that was not WASP or affected by the interests of the minorities we studied" (Higher Education Research Institute, 1982, p.3).

tory racism enabled only highly educated, professional immigrants to enter the United States, and the statistical artifact of such restricted access is now proffered as evidence that Asian education issues do not deserve analysis. Not only is there considerable evidence of educational and occupational segregation (Chun 1980; U.S. Commission on Civil Rights 1979), but the changing demography of Asian immigration will soon enough manifest itself in the educational disadvantage that seems not to be in evidence now.

The Changed Mood

It is appropriate to end my brief litany of minority access issues with a sketch of Asian issues, for it is my thesis that majority perceptions and public policy determine the legitimacy of minority research agendas. When Asian refugees are perceived as a national problem necessitating a solution, a research and service agenda will be hastily constructed and Asian expertise will be solicited and convened. Indians and migrant children no longer enjoy majority support generated by larger political activities, and the BIA can be systematically dismantled by the administration. Secretary of the Interior James Watt is reviled by majority communities for his environmental perspectives, but his even more extreme policies in administering Indian trust responsibilities escape notice in the mainstream press.

It is this fickle public and its role in shaping public policy that was examined by Faustine Jones in her recent *The Changing Mood in America: Eroding Commitment?* (Jones 1977). She concluded that there is

. . . an eroding commitment to blacks, other minorities, and the poor at this time [and a] current resurgence of conservatism throughout the nation, which has negatively affected these groups in their quest to gain the American Creed's promise of equality and justice in their own land (p. 275).

Another critic of societal perceptions of equality is Lorenzo Morris, who has noted that there is

. . . a lesson to be learned from the inevitable imperfections of inequality. That is, that episodes of equal opportunity, or even its preponderance in selected areas of higher education, do not make the system egalitarian. Unfortunately, many critics have been so impressed by the newly erected monuments to equal opportunity that they have failed to recognize that the foundations are the same as those which for centuries have perpetuated a structure of inequality of opportunity (Morris 1979, p. 273).

To those of us who have worked with different political situations, there is always the temptation to hold "liberal" administrations to higher standards of scrutiny than those to which we hold "conservative" administrations. If anything, our disappointment is more severe when "liberals" fail to meet expectations, because our expectations are inevitably higher. There-fore, more nostalgic times are remembered, and the harshness of present realities dulls our sense of how few fundamental improvements happened earlier. If this seems jaded or too caustic, then I plead guilty, for nearly 15 years of civil rights legislation have not substantially improved the condition of minority education, while, ironically, the prevailing illusion of substan-tially increased access has forestalled necessary changes in existing systems. Thus, minorities and other underrepresented groups find themselves un-derserved by programs designed to redress inequities, and ill served by a popular notion that inequities no longer exist.

Institutional Barriers

Governmental and institutional barriers do continue to exist and to reinforce each other. To the extent that federal programs influence institutional be-havior, and to the extent that institutional advocacy influences federal policies, these barriers to fuller participation by minorities form a cycle difficult to halt without specific policy intervention. In the 1960s and 1970s, such intervention was usually initiated by student activists, by litigation, or by comprehensive legislation. None of these alternatives is being employed effectively to bring sufficient pressure to bear on the barriers facing minor-ities in higher education, in part because there is no consensus on the extent of the problems and no evidence of political solutions to these problems. The first move in remedying this situation is to acknowledge the condition as problematic and to examine strategies by which existing bar-riers can be eradicated. It is necessary to outline major structural barriers to increasing minority access and analyze the policy implications of these barriers; in several instances, program initiatives that ignore minority de-mographics predictably failed to improve access for the very groups for whom the legislation was intended. In other cases, institutional failures to make reasonable administrative efforts have adversely affected minority populations. Because these failures in the educational policy process are reflective of a larger societal failure to address minority issues, the final portion of this paper will treat in some detail specific institutional barriers that, in my view, embody higher education's fall from grace.

Those of us who found ourselves in the loyal opposition over the last four years have found both our loyalty and opposition tested in recent events. Those of us who have been professionally committed to the devel-opment of categorical programs have frequently perceived that it was school systems and higher education institutions that were, in large part, the problem. And we relied, perhaps to our detriment on occasion, on federal legislation, because it was easier to try to attack systemic problems from the top rather than from the bottom. Many of us do not have the margin of error available to us to allow change to percolate upward. Moreover, the history of higher education litigation suggests that people who do litigate against institutions have done so because of their perceptions that institutions have not been sensitive to the concerns of historically excluded groups. The history of *Brown* was only one such attempt to open higher education's doors.

Over the years, education legislation has evolved targeting language to focus on the group being excluded—"underrepresented" groups, groups for whom English is not a primary language, "first generation college attenders," "disadvantaged," or in one particularly galling case, "culturally" disadvantaged.[4] These were deliberate attempts to focus resources and efforts on discrete groups and recipients. Yet we have frequently found ourselves frustrated when, having been able to change laws and to impact on the promulgation of regulations, we then faced the insensitivity of the institutions that were the direct recipients of that money.

In the Higher Education Act, recently reauthorized, institutions sought their own legislation, particularly and most notably in the urban grant program. Of course, such a law would necessitate regulations. All laws require that administrative rules be promulgated, and higher education's participation in the normal political process to seek favorable legislation therefore increases the attendant regulations. And it would be unjustifiably modest of the Washington higher education associations to suggest they are without portfolio in influencing regulations. The Higher Education Community Task Forces on Regulations was enormously successful in tailoring regulations to guide the Higher Education Act reauthorization it had so successfully influenced in the first place. Moreover, the associations comment upon and shape proposed rules every day, and do so with an extraordinary advantage over those groups who perceive themselves to have little influence within institutions.

Higher education has lobbied, influenced, and traded—as the rest of Washington has done—but then expected specific exemption. Most recently, higher education sought and received, at least partially, exemption from age discrimination provisions; the associations and institutions pleaded that education was different and therefore deserved exemption. Laura Ford, former assistant director of governmental relations of the American Council on Education, alluded to such exemptions in old age provisions when she advised "greater sensitivity to the moral implications of whatever positions are taken" (Ford 1978-79). To many of us who witnessed the tortured logic employed by colleges to seek their exemption (particularly the often-voiced

---

4. 45 CFR 179.44c (3) ii; 45 CFR 166.13 (a); Education Amendments of 1980, Title IV, Sec. 417D(1)B; 45 CFR 155.1 (a); 45 CFR 159.2 (c).

insistence that *not* to do so would jeopardize places for women and minority faculty), higher education's credibility was cynically compromised.

Examples abound in elementary and secondary education, as well. In the collection of racial and ethnic data so important to those of us who try to measure minority progress, it is the Chief State School Officers who have proved to be the obstacle. One of their activities, under the acronym of CEIS (Committee for Evaluation and Information Systems), has been to beat back efforts at gathering more comprehensive data—including minority or nonminority classes in individual schools.[5] CEIS succeeded in having classroom racial and ethnic composition deleted from the Office for Civil Rights forms, despite the evidence that Hispanic and black children have been increasingly segregated since 1970. Because the review of proposed data gathering activities is such an esoteric, technical enterprise, CEIS has an enormous advantage over advocates for increased racial data efforts; moreover, in the name of "reduced paperwork" or "streamlining bureaucracy," there is a political predisposition to deleting questions that will, in the main, make schools look bad. Therefore, those of us who measure social progress—or, as in the case of desegregation, who measure the lack of social progress—on this issue will not have the means available. We will have to resort to more obtrusive measures because the data are being removed as tools available to us.

Another manifestation of institutions trying to have it both ways is litigation. The *Yeshiva* and *Elkins*[6] cases have shown the extent to which institutions will go in using the judicial system to advance their singular interests. The decision in *Yeshiva* would have us believe that faculty are managers without answering who are the "managed" (Lee 1980-81). In *Elkins,* Maryland attempted to deny state resident status to a foreign student who held a G-4 nonimmigrant card. The Supreme Court held that the foreign student, who had lived in the United States for much of his adult life, could not be held to the presumption that he was never able to become a Maryland resident.

I concede, of course, that litigants should employ whatever honorable theory serves their interest. It is lamentable, though, that higher education does not, as a rule, practice preventive law or self-regulation. Athletics is a shameful aspect of higher education, one that reduces institutions to practices as low as those of corporations who bend rules and exploit political circumstance to their own narrow, commercial interests. And even the most distinguished, thoughtful representatives of higher education, such as those who served on the Sloan Commission, can propose untenable

---

5. *Federal Register,* 46, No. 30 (February 13, 1981), 12232–12233.

6. *National Labor Relations Board v. Yeshiva University,* 440 U.S. 672 (1980); *Toll v. Moreno,* 99 S. Ct. 2044 (1979).

suggestions, most notably the Council for Equal Opportunity in Higher Education. This proposal for short-circuiting the legal process for aggrieved faculty raises serious questions about higher education's motives. As Judges Higginbotham and Edwards have asked, why should higher education be exempted any more than other industries? (Sloan 1980; Edwards 1980).

Higher education has lost its moral cloak in *not* protesting some of the more egregious incidents of federal interference. For example, the Ashbrook appropriations rider precluded school districts from teaching bilingual children with federal funds unless the children were immersed in English classes.[7] I cannot imagine a more flagrant, nationalistic intrusion into curriculum, into pedagogy, or into the classroom. And yet education has not raised its voice in protest. The associations similarly ignored the flouting of law in recent Basic Educational Opportunity Grant (BEOG) rescissions, when $50 and then $80 were lopped off each student's BEOG package—despite elaborate rollback provisions in the law, based on need determinations (Gladieux 1980). I fear the scenario that across-the-board cuts will be made in even larger amounts as an ostensibly equitable economy measure. Higher education, in my view, will have lost its ability to protest these rollbacks by virtue of its acquiescence and silence in earlier actions.

Higher education was also conspicuously silent in minority legislation—e.g., the Tribally Controlled Community College Assistance Act of 1978. Despite the specificity of the legislation, fewer than half of the 20 tribal colleges have received money from the Act. A major impediment has been the requirement that the colleges be "institutions"—and the statute requires accreditation as a prerequisite to being an institution—and yet these schools are not accredited by virtue of their rural isolation and their newness (Olivas 1982b). Dupont Circle has never raised its voice in protest, nor has it been helpful in attempts to get this legislation reconsidered.

Are "new arrangements" desirable? In the rush to secure resources, institutions are exploring new arrangements with industry, the military, and governments—and only extremists would argue that such ties are per se wrong. Higher education has historically and honorably allied itself with commerce and national security, and educators have a responsibility to serve and enrich the societies in which they exist. What is essential, however—and what is not being thoroughly ventilated—is the extent to which institutions sacrifice their principles in allying themselves with interests detrimental to free inquiry and scholarship. Higher education will not come to this debate with clean hands, as the many examples already noted suggest, and one could mount persuasive arguments that the academy has always been "compromised" in its historical, and frequently secretive, collaboration with the military and corporations.

---

7. H. R. 7998, August 27, 1980.

I am no Utopian or Luddite and do not reject as unpalatable all corporate and military support, inasmuch as industry and the military draw trained personnel directly from education. Even if many actions are shortsighted— as I believe industry raids on science and engineering faculty to be— generous corporate support is essential for long-term stability in research and training. However, industry exacts far too much for its modest investments, and too often "creams off the top" of students and faculty, leaving nonscience majors, disadvantaged students, and liberal arts research to their own devices. Although the military and corporate sectors have vested interests in assuming general institutional health, they rarely see beyond narrow, selfish ends. Increasing competition between universities and the military for the traditional college-age cohort will severely test the tentative truce in effect since the Vietnam war years. Higher education and corporations surely share a trait in common: neither sector plans for long-range development. I have cited several prominent examples of this myopia as it relates to service to minority communities.

These remarks will surely seem an indictment of societal and institutional behavior. I do not urge the radical Right to seize on such a trenchant analysis as evidence to argue their own perspective—that governmental involvement in education is inappropriate. To argue from my disappointment that the federal role in education is unnecessary would cynically distort my premise. The federal and state roles in funding and monitoring education are essential and represent the major opportunity to improve access for historically excluded groups.

My hope for improvement lies in demographics and the good will of educators at the institutional and school levels. However, I find it anomalous that education seeks to be exempted from rules for which no societally legitimate exemption could be justified. Education seeks to have it both ways, and the regulatory process is one check on the frequently undeserved influence that education enjoys. There are, of course, governmental excesses at the federal and especially the state level. Nonetheless, I remain convinced that the education industry is no more progressive and deserving of public policy exemption or favor than are other established sectors of society. Its charge is greater and its responsibilities are surely fundamental, but its abuse of trust is just as surely a greater disappointment.

References

Astin, A., "Academic Administration: The Hard Core of Sexism in Academe," *UCLA Educator,* 19 (Spring 1977), 60–66.

Barriers to Higher Education (New York: College Entrance Examination Board, 1971).

Chun, K., "The Myth of Asian American Success and Its Educational Ramifications," *IRCD Bulletin,* 15 (1980), 1–12.

Edwards, H., *Higher Education and the Unholy Crusade against Governmental Regulation* (Cambridge: Institute for Educational Management, 1980).

Ford, L., "The Implications of the Age Discrimination in Education Act Amendments of 1978 for Colleges and Universities," *Journal of College and University Law,* 5 (1978-79), 161–210.

Gilford, D., and J. Snyder, *Women and Minority PhD's in the 1970's* (Washington, D.C.: National Academy of Sciences, 1977).

Gladieux, L., "What Has Congress Wrought?" *Change,* 12 (October 1980), 25–31.

Haynes, L., *A Conceptual Examination of Desegregation in Higher Education* (Washington, D.C.: Institute for Services to Education, 1978).

Higher Education Research Institute, *Final Report of the Commission on the Higher Education of Minorities* (Los Angeles: Higher Education Research Institute, 1982).

Institute for the Study of Educational Policy, *Equal Educational Opportunity* (Washington, D.C.: Institute for the Study of Educational Policy, 1980).

Jones, F., *The Changing Mood in America: Eroding Commitment?* (Washington, D.C.: Institute for the Study of Educational Policy, 1977).

Lee, B., "Faculty Role in Academic Governance and the Managerial Exclusion: Impact of the Yeshiva University Decision," *Journal of College and University Law,* 7 (1980-81), 222–266.

Lopez, R., et al., *Chicanos in Higher Education: Status and Issues* (Los Angeles: UCLA Chicano Studies Center, 1976).

Morris, L., *Elusive Equality* (Washington, D.C.: Howard University Press, 1979).

Olivas, M., *The Dilemma of Access* (Washington, D.C.: Howard University Press, 1979).

Olivas, M., "Federal Higher Education Policy: The Case of Hispanics," *Educational Evaluation of Policy Analysis,* 4, 3 (1982a).

Olivas, M., "Indian, Chicano, and Puerto Rican Colleges: Status and Issues," *Bilingual Review,* 11, 1 (1982b), 36–58.

Olivas M., *Research on Hispanic Education: Students, Finance, and Governance* (Stanford: Institute for Finance and Governance, 1981).

Olivas, M., and S. Hill, "Hispanic Participation in Postsecondary Education," in National Center for Education Statistics, *The Condition of Education for Hispanic Americans* (Washington, D.C.: National Center for Education Statistics, 1980), 117–216.

Sloan Commission on Government and Higher Education, *A Program for Renewed Partnership* (Cambridge: Ballinger, 1980).

U.S. Commission on Civil Rights, *Civil Rights Issues of Asian and Pacific Americans* (Washington, D.C.: U.S. Commission on Civil Rights, 1979).

Wood, D., "Academic Women's Studies Programs: A Case of Organizational Innovation," *Journal of Higher Education,* 52, 2 (1981), 155–172.

Response by Alfred L. Moyé

Olivas's view is justifiably pessimistic given the conditions of education vis à vis the federal government. It is indeed ironic that programs that were established, in part, in the name of defense are now being dismantled in support of defense.

From its founding, this country knew that an educated citizenry was necessary if democracy were to succeed. How much more important is education in preserving democracy in an era when the demands of a more complex, technical society are infinitely greater than even 50 years ago?

In *Higher Learning in the Nation's Service*, Boyer and Hechinger make reference to the military "where equipment has already become more sophisticated than the available labor force and where buying more hardware seems unwise unless accompanied by at least a comparable investment in the people who will have to use it."[1] The writers do not single out the military for criticism but use examples to underscore a point that the change from a machine-based manufacturing society to a high technology, service-oriented economy requires a more educated workforce to meet the needs of the nation.

While Olivas believes that optimism is unwarranted for the reasons he cites, I believe that more, not less, must be done, even in the absence of government support. Additionally, efforts must be extended beyond the scope of programs of the past decade to include services to an adult population which will dominate the workforce by 1990 and which is undereducated.

There will be a decline in the 18-24 age group of 23.3 percent by 1997,[2] and by the year 2000, the largest age group in America will be 30-to-44-year-olds.[3] Recent estimates are that 47 percent of all people aged 16-21 (approximately 12 million) are functionally illiterate.[4] Clearly, then, meeting the educational needs of the adult learner must be a high national priority if citizens are to reach their potential and if a quality workforce is to be maintained.

Unfortunately public and institutional policies have favored the traditional student, and the education of adults has been a secondary activity.

For example, New York has 5.6 million people over 16 years old who

---

1. Carnegie Foundation for the Advancement of Teaching, *Higher Learning in the National Service*. Washington, D.C., Carnegie, 1981.

2. Carnegie Council on Policy Studies in Higher Education, *Three Thousand Futures*. (San Francisco, Jossey-Bass, 1980), p. 37.

3. Cross, K. Patricia. *Adults as Learners*. (San Francisco, Jossey-Bass, 1981).

4. Carnegie Council on Policy Studies in Higher Education, cited by Chapman.

have left school before graduation; yet only one-eighth of one percent of New York state's elementary, secondary, and continuing education budget is allocated for education of this population. The figures for higher education are likewise skewed toward the younger traditional students.[5]

It is also known that the majority of the adult education programs that do exist do not serve the undereducated. "Virtually every study undertaken to describe volunteer adult learners concludes it is the well-educated who rush to take advantage of education opportunity, while the poorly educated stay away in droves."[6] Also, we find that white adults participate in education at nearly twice the rate of blacks. The percentages for Hispanics are even lower.[7]

In defining the adult learner as a new population to be served, I am not suggesting that we abandon programs designed to serve the young. On the contrary, it would be a national disaster to retreat from the advances of the past decade. State and federal student aid programs provide access and choice, provided they are not targeted to students on the basis of merit, as Derek Bok advocates in his 1982 annual report to the Harvard Board of Overseers. On the other hand, the adult learner should not be systematically excluded from participation because of an inability to attend on a greater-than-half-time basis.

The academic support programs that the government has funded in the past decade must also be continued. But I think some restructuring may be needed to focus more on courses of study that will prepare the disadvantaged for emerging fields and fields of high national need in which minorities are underrepresented. These areas include engineering, math, science, languages, computer science, telecommunications and medicine.

In order to serve adequately the educational needs of adults in the workforce, new relationships must be established between institutions of higher education and employers. Currently, private industry spends between $30 and $40 billion a year on education and training. Obviously, the private sector is concerned about and involved in the education and training of its employees, and higher education is just one segment of the educational enterprise. But the maximum benefit will be achieved with cooperation between the two sectors.

Financial arrangements must be made to support adults who wish to pursue their education in noncollegiate settings. Here I wish to distinguish between training or retraining for a specific job and general education. The

---

5. *New York Times*, "Adult Learning: Better Late than Never." February 14, 1982, p. E-7.

6. Cross, K. Patricia. "Emerging Issues in the Learning Society." Speech before the Boston Conference on Encouraging Part-Time and Adult Enrollments, February 16, 1982.

7. Cross, ibid.

corporate world is responsible for the training needs of its employees, but there is merit in using public monies to support general education, even when it occurs away from the campus.

Advanced technology can provide access to the rurally isolated, the homebound, the shift worker, etc.; and such educational efforts should be supported by federal and state funds, as long as these programs deliver an educational service.

"If academic institutions intend to offer continuing education in the future, they will have to develop telecommunications 'courseware' for cable television and home computers," according to Calvin B. T. Lee, a vice president of the Prudential Insurance Company of America. He urged colleges and universities to develop "courseware packages," which could include "a magnetic tape or floppy disc, a set of microfiche cards and, most commonly, a set of printed materials."[8]

I submit that it would be appropriate for the business world to pool financial resources to support joint ventures by a group of institutions to develop the "coursewares" that can be utilized by business and industry. The capital investment to bring the coursewares to their employees would be minuscule when measured against the impact on the workforce.

The decline in graduate education is reaching crisis proportion for society as a whole, but particularly for minorities, and requires new incentives to stimulate growth. A recent Council of Graduate Schools study showed a 1 percent decline in graduate enrollment in fall 1981, compared with 1980. However, the 1980 graduate enrollment survey showed a drop in first-year graduate enrollments of 7 percent for blacks, 2.8 percent for Hispanics, and 8.5 percent for native Americans.

The magnitude of the problem is illustrated by a recent article in the *Chronicle of Higher Education*. Since the Bakke case in 1978, the University of California at Davis Medical School has been accepting fewer applications from minorities. "Only 3.8 percent of the minority group students who applied to Davis were accepted last fall, compared with 5.1 percent in 1980 and 8.5 percent in 1979."

At Stanford, "The signs look just terrible, especially for blacks," according to Gerald Lieberman, vice provost. "The numbers of minority group students admitted to doctoral programs in the humanities and sciences at Stanford for next fall [will] be fifty percent lower than last fall." Mr. Lieberman reported also that Princeton anticipated a decline in minority graduate enrollment as applications from blacks dropped 25 percent.[9]

With some exceptions, higher education remains committed to equity in

---

8. *Chronicle of Higher Education*, June 9, 1982, p. 3.
9. *Chronicle of Higher Education*, May 19, 1982, p. 3.

graduate education. However, new approaches are needed to increase the numbers of minorities in graduate and professional programs.

> Equity is not merely a concession to those who have historically been denied the chance to take part. Rather it stands as a viable strategy to ensure that America's most treasured resource, the capabilities of its people, is not squandered. Educational equity, in short, is a national investment.[10]

The reasons for decline in graduate enrollment are many. But in business, science, and engineering the attractiveness of high salaries is luring would-be doctoral candidates into industry. The long-range effect will be a decline in basic research and decline in professionals with research skills.

To avoid problems of trained manpower shortages of the magnitude that existed, at least in perception, in the late 1950s an intervention strategy is needed today. The private sector could encourage graduate education by designing new arrangements to facilitate graduate study. Universities could cooperate by permitting part-time study (as some do not currently permit) and by adopting flexible schedules to meet the needs of working, graduate students. Also, graduate study could be encouraged if legitimate, independent research, done on the job, were considered appropriate for thesis recognition.

The federal government could provide incentives to firms that significantly support its employees who pursue graduate education.

It is not easy to convince those who have been economically disadvantaged to delay entry into the workforce. However, we may be able to achieve the desired results by designing arrangements that will facilitate the employed adult's pursuit of a terminal degree. It is in the best interest of industry, the institution, and government to cooperate in the effort.

Another reason for decline in graduate enrollment is the lack of employment opportunities for those who receive the terminal degree—the bulk of whom aspire to university teaching. The prospects for university employment have been significantly reduced because of academic retrenchment and the change in the mandatory retirement age. To encourage people, especially the disadvantaged, to pursue graduate education in this period, it is recommended that the federal government establish an "intellectual corps" (for lack of a better term) to provide employment in research laboratories or teaching positions at carefully selected institutions, which can be strengthened by the presence of those selected to the corps. This would provide an acceptable alternative for those waiting for positions to open up.

---

10. Black Higher Education Fact Sheet, No. 11, May 1982. National Advisory Council on Blacks in Higher Education and Black Colleges and Universities.

In discussing new populations and new arrangements, I recommend consideration of the following thoughts:

1. The educational needs of undereducated adult learners should be made a high national priority.

2. Business and higher education should cooperate in meeting these needs.

3. Financial assistance and academic support should be provided for adults pursuing general education in collegiate and noncollegiate settings and by nontraditional delivery systems. The ultimate test should be whether educational services are provided.

4. Higher education must take advantage of technological advances and develop telecommunication coursewares to make education more accessible to adults.

5. Industry gains from a better-educated workforce and should be encouraged to support programs that serve their employees.

6. The crisis in graduate education hits the disadvantaged hardest. The federal government has a primary role in maintaining the research capability of the nation and should take steps to offset the current decline.

References

Black Higher Education Fact Sheet, No. 11, May 1982. National Advisory Council on Blacks in Higher Education and Black Colleges and Universities.

Carnegie Council on Policy Studies in Higher Education, *Three Thousand Futures* (San Francisco: Jossey-Bass, 1980), p. 37.

Carnegie Foundation for the Advancement of Teaching, *Higher Learning in the National Service.* Washington, D.C.: Carnegie, 1981.

Chapman, Dale T., "Adult Learner and the Public Interest." Paper prepared for the American Council on Education, Washington, D.C., April 19, 1982.

Chronicle of Higher Education, May 19, 1982, p. 3.

Chronicle of Higher Education, June 9, 1982, p. 3.

Cross, K. Patricia, *Adults as Learners* (San Francisco, Jossey-Bass, 1981).

Cross, K. Patricia, "Emerging Issues in the Learning Society." Speech before the Boston Conference on Encouraging Part-Time and Adult Enrollments, February 16, 1982.

New York Times, "Adult Learning: Better Late than Never." February 14, 1982, p. E-7.

Minorities in Higher Education

Alexander W. Astin

The following pages are reproduced from the *Final Report of the Commission on the Higher Education of Minorities,* by the Higher Education Research Institute, Inc. (Los Angeles, California), which was distributed to participants in advance of the conference. The report is part of an overall study, *Minorities in American Higher Education,* by Alexander W. Astin (San Francisco: Jossey-Bass Inc., Publishers, 1982), copyright © 1982 by the Commission on the Higher Education of Minorities. The excerpt is printed in this book by permission of the copyright holder.

Introduction

The recommendations presented here are based on findings from a study of the higher education status of four of the principal disadvantaged racial and ethnic minorities in the United States—Blacks, Chicanos, Puerto Ricans, and American Indians. During the fall of 1978, when the project was in the planning stage, HERI and the Ford Foundation jointly selected a national commission, structured to include at least one member of each of the four minority groups, to serve as advisory board and policy arm for the project.

The commissioners bring to their task a set of shared value premises that they wish to make explicit to the reader. We believe that these premises are widely held among the four peoples who are the main concern of this report, and that the principles they embody are consistent with ideals of social equity that have an enduring appeal for people of all conditions and nationalities. By stating these premises forthrightly, the commission hopes to aid the reader in understanding the way in which our inquiry has been structured, the significance of the findings and of our interpretations, and the validity of the recommended actions.

Our value premises can be stated as follows:

- Education is a value and a right that is unequally distributed in U.S. society.
- Blacks, Chicanos, Puerto Ricans, and American Indians are major groups with longstanding unmet claims on U.S. education. These claims concern not only the amount of schooling received, but also its quality, scope, and content.
- Redressing inequality in higher education is not only an essential component of any significant effort to guarantee to these groups full participation in U.S. society, but also a goal worth pursuing in its own right.
- The attainment of full participation in higher education for these groups may in the short run require that financial and other resources be allocated in a manner governed more by considerations of the magnitude of existing inequality than by considerations of the proportions these groups represent in the total U.S. population.
- U.S. society as a whole has practical and moral interests in the achievement of this goal.

None of these premises, it should be emphasized, assumes that any of the four groups need give up its cultural distinctiveness, languages, or values in the process of gaining full access to higher education and full social and economic participation in American life.

The principal purposes of the project were to examine the recent progress, current status, and future prospects of Blacks, Chicanos, Puerto Ricans, and American Indians in higher education and to formulate recommendations aimed at furthering the educational development of these groups. Although other racial and ethnic minorities can also be viewed as having unmet claims on U.S. higher education, these four groups were chosen for study because of their size, the gravity of their economic and educational disadvantagement, and their original experience of forced incorporation into U.S. society.

The major functions of the commission were to advise the HERI staff on proposed and completed studies, to give guidance in the interpretation of findings and the formulation of recommendations, and to assist with the dissemination of both findings and recommendations to policy makers, practitioners, and the general public. Subcommittees comprising both commissioners and staff members were formed to deal with specific issues such as governmental programs, the quality of the data used in the project, and minority women. A major outcome of the commission's involvement in the project was the decision to produce, in addition to the present document, five reports—an overall summary report on the entire project and four separate reports on each of the minority groups. It was felt that these four "subreports" would provide an opportunity to discuss in detail the history and special problems of each minority group.

The full commission met eight times during the project period: on February 25–26, 1979, June 1–2, 1979, and October 5–6, 1979, at Los Angeles; on January 12–13, 1980, at San Antonio; on March 21–22, 1980, in New York; on November 7–8, 1980 at Los Angeles; on April 10–12, 1981, at Ramona (California); and on July 19–21, 1981, again at Los Angeles. These meetings gave commissioners and staff members an opportunity to debate and discuss the issues, to review and revise the study design, to assess the quality of available data, to suggest interpretations of empirical findings, and to draft recommendations. At the San Antonio and New York meetings, which focused on the special problems of Chicanos and Puerto Ricans, respectively, the commissioners met with local people involved with programs targeted for these two groups. The April and July meetings in 1981 were designed to review draft sections of the reports.

Context of the Study

When this project was initiated in late 1978, concern for the plight of disadvantaged minorities—which had its genesis in the civil rights movement of the 1950s and which had been strong in the 1960s and early 1970s—was on the wane. National attention was being absorbed instead by such issues as inflation, unemployment, the energy crisis, and the defense budget. In addition, an increasing number of socially and economically disadvantaged groups, including the elderly, women workers, and the handicapped, had begun to assert their claims to equitable treatment, financial resources, and compensatory services.

More recent developments on the political scene have not been reassuring. As this statement is being drafted, the Reagan Administration is recommending—and Congress has accepted—major cuts in the federal budget, the impact of which will fall heavily on education and on minority-oriented programs.

This mood shift has been as apparent in higher education as in other sectors of American society. During the 1960s and early 1970s, partly as a result of racial protests on the campus and in the community, many colleges and universities accepted changes—open admissions, recruitment of minorities, establishment of ethnic studies programs—that acknowledged the unmet claims of minorities in the United States and the inequitable treatment they had received from the educational system. However, concern over rising costs, along with the fear that projected declines in the college-age population during the 1980s and 1990s would severely erode institutional revenues, led to cost-consciousness and calls for retrenchment. These newer programs, many of which had been initiated on an experimental basis or supported by special outside funding from foundations or the federal government, were especially vulnerable to funding reductions or to elimination. Adding to the budgetary anxiety was apparent public skepticism about the value of higher education, particularly its relative costs and benefits.

A recent report of the National Forum on Learning in the American Future makes it clear that higher education has begun to subordinate minority issues to other concerns.* Respondents to this survey—including 1,556 "policy decision makers, educators, and scholars"—were asked to indicate the relative importance of a number of issues both as present and as future goals. Although minority issues were generally given high priority as present goals, they were rated very low among future goals; this was especially true for such matters as promoting affirmative action for minority advancement, recruiting and training minority-group members for managerial and professional positions, providing compensatory educational op-

---

* R. Glover and B. Gross, *Report on the National Forum on Learning in the American Future: Future Needs and Goals for Adult Learning, 1980–2000* (New York: Future Directions for a Learning Society, The College Board, 1979).

portunities to the disadvantaged, and enabling bilingual minorities to study their own cultures and languages.

If the current attitude of some educators toward minority issues is one of benign neglect or indifference, the attitudes expressed by some litigants through the federal courts may be characterized as overtly hostile. The U.S. Supreme Court's *DeFunis* (1974) and *Bakke* (1978) cases, for example, reflect a growing public view that higher education institutions have "gone too far" in their attempts to accommodate the special needs of minorities. Similar attitude changes are evidenced by increased resistance to court-ordered busing as a means of ending racial segregation in the public schools.

The prevailing political climate regarding minority issues is illustrated in a recent column by British journalist Christopher Hitchens, writing for the predominantly American audience of *The Nation* (June 13, 1981):

> The status of Black Americans seems hardly to be an issue any more. A depressing series in *The New York Times* reveals what a low priority the question has become, and sees Blacks bracing themselves for a period of neglect and isolation. I well remember, last autumn, during your election campaign, attending a liberal fund-raising party in New York City. Moving around the glittering apartment, I noticed two things. First, there were no Black guests. Second, all those handing round drinks and canapés were black. On a liberal occasion, it seemed to me that you could have one or the other, but not both, of those phenomena. I asked the host about it. He looked puzzled for a moment and then said, "Oh, *that*. Out of style."

As previously stated, the principal purposes of this project were to examine the past gains, current status, and future prospects of Blacks, Chicanos, Puerto Ricans, and American Indians in higher education and to formulate recommendations aimed at furthering the educational development of these groups. To provide a strong empirical basis for policy recommendations, the study was originally designed to concentrate on two areas: first, on a description of the current and recent situation of the four minority groups with respect to their access to higher education, choice of institutions and of fields of study, and degree attainment; and second, on an analysis of the factors that influence the access and attainment of these minority groups. During the course of the study, the commission overseeing the project added a third major area of activity: an analysis of controversial issues relating to the higher education of minorities.

The specific questions addressed under each of these three major categories of research activity are listed below:

Educational Access, Choice, and Attainment

- To what extent are Blacks, Chicanos, Puerto Ricans, and American Indians represented at various points in the educational pipeline between secondary school and completion of advanced training? Where are the major leakage points in this pipeline?
- What is the representation of each of these four minority groups by field of study and type of institution?
- How has the representation of each minority group changed since the mid-1960s?

Factors Influencing Educational Development

- How are the educational access and attainment of minority students influenced by family background, socioeconomic status, and personal characteristics?
- What features or characteristics of educational institutions and programs (for example, type of high school, type of higher education institution, student peer groups, faculty attitudes, special institutional programs) are most critical in affecting the progress of minority students?
- How is the progress of minority students affected by the type of financial aid they receive during undergraduate and graduate training?
- Which governmental programs seem to be the most effective and which the least effective in facilitating minority progress in higher education?

Controversial Issues

- To what extent are minorities afforded equal access to higher education? Is "equality of access" more a myth than a reality?
- How valid is the current popular stereotype of the "overeducated American"? What implications for minority progress in higher education does acceptance of this stereotype have?
- In what way does standardized testing, as currently used, impede the educational development of minorities? How can standardized testing be employed to contribute to educational development?
- How do the meritocratic aspects of the U.S. higher education system affect minority progress?

The first two categories of research activities—"educational access, choice, and attainment" and "factors influencing educational development"— were approached by means of a series of analyses of empirical data. While considerable use was made of existing data sources, a substantial amount of new data was also collected. The third major category of project activity— "controversial issues"—was accomplished by means of a series of essays drawing upon the existing literature and, in some instances, upon relevant empirical data.

Data Sources

Empirical studies performed by the commission staff involved the use of several resources, including data from public documents; unpublished data from outside agencies; and data collected especially for the project and, in most cases, involving questionnaire surveys. Data pertaining to the educational access and attainment of minorities were obtained from several public and private sources, including the U.S. Bureau of the Census, the Commission on Civil Rights, the Office for Civil Rights, the National Center for Education Statistics, the National Science Foundation, the National Academy of Sciences (National Research Council), the College Entrance Examination Board (Educational Testing Service), the American College Testing Program, and the Cooperative Institutional Research Program of the American Council on Education and the University of California, Los Angeles. These data provided the principal basis for the commission's analysis of the educational pipeline for minorities (from the high school years through completion of advanced training), the representation of minorities in different fields, and recent trends in minority representation both by level and by field.

Factors influencing the educational development of minority students were assessed primarily through longitudinal data from the Cooperative Institutional Research Program. The principal source for these analyses was a nine-year follow-up of 1971 entering freshmen, conducted especially for this project during the spring of 1980. In order to obtain an accurate picture of the persistence rates of minorities during this nine-year interval, a number of follow-up procedures were used to improve response rates.

Another source of student data involved a national sample of minority students who had received graduate fellowships for doctoral study from the Ford Foundation between 1969 and 1976. To estimate the impact of this fellowship award itself, a "natural experiment" was conducted whereby the same follow-up questionnaire sent to the 1971 freshmen was sent to all Ford Fellows who began their undergraduate studies in 1971 and to a control group of applicants for the Ford graduate awards who had not received the award and who had also entered college in 1971.

Data on faculty and staff were also collected via a national survey of academic personnel working in the same institutions attended by the 1971 sample and a survey designed to tap the experiences and perceptions of minority educators.

These data on students and faculty were supplemented by additional data on the institutions' finances, enrollments, physical plants, and admissions policies, and other environmental information obtained from public and private sources.

Data Analyses

Descriptive studies of the educational access and attainment of minority undergraduates were obtained from published tabulations of several of the data sources described above as well as through special tabulations of these same data sources conducted by the project staff. Analyses of factors influencing minority students' educational development generally involved a two-stage procedure. In the first stage, an attempt was made to adjust for the fact that students entering different types of institutions and different types of programs frequently have dissimilar entering characteristics. Thus in the first stage an attempt was made to control statistically for initial differences in entering student characteristics such as demographic factors (sex, race and ethnicity, age), socioeconomic background (parental education, income, and occupation), high school activities and achievements, plans and aspirations, and values and attitudes. Once these characteristics had been controlled, the second stage in the analysis was performed to estimate the impact of institutional type, financial aid, and other college environmental factors.

Limitations of the Data

It should be emphasized that conclusions based on the commission's analyses of empirical data must be tempered with the recognition that most of the data sources suffered in varying degrees from technical limitations. Among the most frequently encountered types of limitations were inadequate racial and ethnic definitions, small sample sizes, nonrepresentativeness, and low survey response rates. The best data currently available pertain to Black students, whereas the most serious deficiencies occur in data on Puerto Ricans and American Indians.

The Limits of Higher Education

Higher education was chosen as the focus of this study because the Ford Foundation and the persons associated with the project believe that it contributes to the social and economic well-being of individuals and to the political resources and strength of groups within U.S. society. Blacks, Chicanos, Puerto Ricans, and American Indians all suffer from powerlessness, and higher education is clearly one of the main routes whereby individuals can attain positions of economic and political power. Further, the quality of life in general can be improved through higher education, which expands employment options and contributes to greater geographic mobility. Finally, higher education can enrich leisure by exposing the individual to a wide range of experiences in the arts, music, literature, history, science, and technology.

But higher education is by no means a panacea for all the problems that confront disadvantaged minorities in the United States. Vestiges of prejudice may persist in the minds of many Americans for years to come, no matter how many minority students complete higher education programs. Perhaps more significant is the fact that many of the educational problems facing these groups occur prior to higher education, at the elementary and secondary levels. Indeed, the results of this study dramatize the need for a much more concerted national effort to upgrade the quality of elementary and secondary education for minorities. Although it is true that higher education can play some role in this process through the selection and training of administrators and teachers in the lower schools, many of the problems of minority education are probably beyond the control of higher education. While the commission believes that this reality does not relieve the higher education system of the responsibility for doing the best job possible with those minority students who manage to enter academic institutions, it also recognizes that solving the problems of precollegiate education for minorities will require the sustained efforts of federal, state, and local governments.

The Educational Pipeline

Much of the technical effort of the project was directed at gathering and synthesizing the best available data on the representation of minorities in higher education. As was pointed out in the discussion of data limitations, several problems arose in connection with this effort. For instance, some of the sources used report data for the general category "Hispanic," rather than separately for different Hispanic subgroups. Therefore, many of the figures for Chicanos and Puerto Ricans reported here are estimates based on the known fact that the former constitute 60 percent of the Hispanic population in the United States, and the latter 15 percent. Another problem is the paucity of data on American Indians; thus, estimates for this minority group may not be accurate and should be treated with caution.

Given these strictures, the following sections give the best estimates possible of the representation of the four racial and ethnic minority groups by level in the educational system, their representation by field of study, and recent trends in the representation of minorities.

By Level

If one views the educational system as a kind of pipeline leading ultimately to positions of leadership and influence in our society, it is possible to identify five major "leakage" points at which disproportionately large numbers of minority group members drop out of the pipeline: completion of high school, entry to college, completion of college, entry to graduate or professional school, and completion of graduate or professional school. The loss of minorities at these five transition points accounts for their substantial underrepresentation in high-level positions. Figure 1 gives an overview of the educational pipeline for all four minority groups under study and for Whites.

High School Graduation. A substantial proportion of minority students leave the educational system before they even complete secondary school, thus severely handicapping their efforts to attain higher levels of education and to avail themselves of a greater range of career options. For instance, the high school dropout rate for Blacks is approximately 28 percent (compared with a rate of about 17 percent for Whites), and this attrition occurs throughout the high school years. Close to half (45 percent) of Chicanos and Puerto Ricans never finish high school, and this attrition begins in the junior high school years and continues through the high school years. Finally, although data are sparse, it appears that approximately 45 percent of American Indian students leave high school before graduation.

College Entry. With the exception of American Indians, those students who manage to complete high school enter college at about the same rate as Whites. Among high school graduates of each racial and ethnic group, approximately 45 percent of Whites and Puerto Ricans, 40 percent of Blacks and Chicanos, and 31 percent of American Indians enroll in college. (The figure for Puerto Ricans may be inflated, because it is based on data from the years when the City University of New York had a more open admissions policy. Since a majority of the Puerto Ricans who are residents of the continental United States live in New York City, they benefited particularly from this policy, which has since been modified.)

Baccalaureate Attainment. Of those who enter college, Whites are much more likely to complete the baccalaureate within the traditional four-year period than are minority students. According to the National Longitudinal Study, 34 percent of the Whites, 24 percent of the Blacks, 16 percent of the

Figure 1. The Educational Pipeline for minorities.

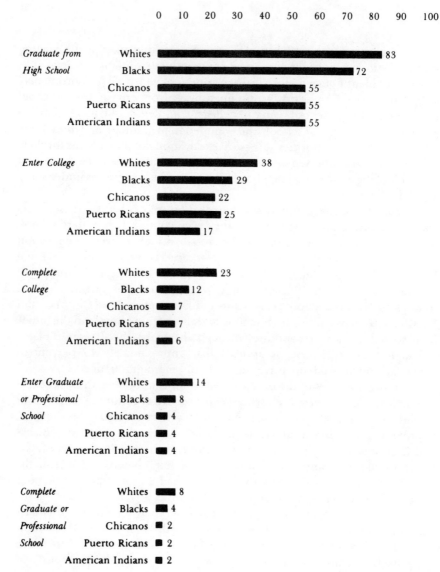

Percent of Cohort

0   10   20   30   40   50   60   70   80   90   100

Graduate from   Whites   83
High School   Blacks   72
                   Chicanos 55
                   Puerto Ricans 55
                   American Indians 55

Enter College   Whites   38
                   Blacks   29
                   Chicanos 22
                   Puerto Ricans 25
                   American Indians 17

Complete   Whites   23
College   Blacks   12
                   Chicanos 7
                   Puerto Ricans 7
                   American Indians 6

Enter Graduate   Whites   14
or Professional Blacks   8
School   Chicanos 4
                   Puerto Ricans 4
                   American Indians 4

Complete   Whites   8
Graduate or   Blacks   4
Professional   Chicanos 2
School   Puerto Ricans 2
                   American Indians 2

American Indians, and 13 percent of the Hispanics who entered college in 1972 had completed the baccalaureate by 1976. In all likelihood, these differences are attributable in part to the high concentration of both Hispanics and American Indians in community colleges. Although three-fourths of community college entrants indicate as freshmen that they intend to get at least a bachelor's degree,* their chances of actually transferring to a senior institution and completing the baccalaureate are slim. Even after taking into account their generally poorer academic preparation, one finds that regardless of race and ethnicity community college students are substantially less likely than are four-year-college entrants to complete four undergraduate years.**

Looking at baccalaureate completion rates beyond the four-year span, one finds that approximately 56 percent of White freshmen, 51 percent of Black freshmen, 42 percent of Puerto Rican freshmen, 40 percent of Chicano freshmen, and 39 percent of American Indian freshmen eventually receive the bachelor's degree. Again, the high concentration of American Indians, Chicanos, and Puerto Ricans in community colleges during the early undergraduate years contributes significantly to their higher baccalaureate attrition rates.

Graduate and Professional School Entry. According to recent data from the U.S. Office for Civil Rights, the transition from undergraduate college to graduate or professional school does not seem to be a major leakage point for minorities; the ratio of the number of first-year graduate students to the number of baccalaureate recipients during the same year was roughly similar for all groups. It should be emphasized, however, that the first-year graduate enrollment figures for minorities may be inflated by delayed entrants (that is, those who do not enroll for advanced training directly after completing the baccalaureate but delay their entry for some period) and the very large proportion of minority students who pursue master's degrees in education.

Advanced Degree Attainment. Although minority students who manage to complete the baccalaureate may not be at a disadvantage when it comes to enrolling in graduate or professional school, they are less likely than White students to complete their advanced training. Approximately 45 percent of Blacks, 52 percent of Chicanos and Puerto Ricans and 48 percent of American Indians drop out before completing their graduate or professional degrees. The comparable figure for Whites is 41 percent.

Summary. The following conclusions can be drawn about the educational pipeline for minorities:

* A. W. Astin, M. R. King, and G. T. Richardson, *The American Freshman: National Norms for Fall 1980* (Los Angeles: UCLA, 1980).
** A. W. Astin, *Preventing Students from Dropping Out* (San Francisco: Jossey-Bass, 1975).

- All four of the minority groups under consideration in this study are increasingly underrepresented at each higher level of degree attainment: high school completion, baccalaureate attainment, and advanced degree attainment.
- Minority underrepresentation is attributable not only to greater than average attrition rates from secondary school, undergraduate college, and graduate and professional school, but also to disproportionately high losses in the transition from high school to college.
- Blacks fall midway between Whites and the three other minority groups in terms of their ability to survive to the end of the educational pipeline.
- The single most important factor contributing to the severe under-representation of Chicanos, Puerto Ricans, and American Indians is their extremely high rate of attrition from secondary school. The second most important factor is their greater than average attrition from undergraduate colleges (particularly community colleges).

By Field

To examine the representation of the four minorities in various fields of study at successive degree levels, the project staff defined ten categories of major fields. Each category was selected either because it is a prerequisite for a high-level career, because it is chosen by a large proportion of students, or because it fulfills both these criteria. The ten categories, which together accounted for about 90 percent of the baccalaureates awarded in the United States in 1978–79, were: allied health; arts and humanities; biological science; business; education; engineering; prelaw; premedicine and predentistry; physical sciences and mathematics; and the social sciences.

It should be pointed out that all four minority groups will tend to be underrepresented in all fields at all levels, because the total proportion who survive to each level is low; and that the underrepresentation in a given field will be even greater if relatively few survivors choose that field.

Among entering freshmen, minorities are underrepresented in all ten categories of fields except the social sciences and education. In addition, Black freshmen are only slightly underrepresented among those naming allied health as a probable major, and are overrepresented among those naming business as a probable major. Moreover, the underrepresentation of minorities increases at each higher level of the educational pipeline. Thus all four minority groups are substantially underrepresented among both baccalaureate recipients and doctorate recipients in all fields. (The only possible exceptions to this generalization are education and the social sciences, where

Blacks seem to be only slightly underrepresented, and American Indians do not seem to be underrepresented.) The field categories in which the four minorities are most severely underrepresented are engineering, biological science, and physical science and mathematics. To achieve proportionate representation in these fields at the doctorate level, the number of minority doctorates would have to increase from four- to sevenfold. The field categories in which minorities are least severely underrepresented (other than education) are the social sciences, law, and medicine. Proportionate representation in these fields could be achieved by doubling the number of minority degree-recipients.

Generally speaking, the factor that best explains minority under-representation in various fields—especially the natural sciences, engineering, and the social sciences—is the poor academic preparation that minority students receive at the precollegiate level.

Recent Trends

Although minority underrepresentation increases at each higher level of the educational pipeline and is especially severe in the sciences and engineering, the last two decades have witnessed dramatic increases in minority representation at all levels of the educational pipeline and in virtually all fields. These increases are attributable in large part to the civil rights movement of the late 1950s and the 1960s, to the Civil Rights Act of 1964, and to the initiation during the 1960s of a number of social programs aimed directly at increasing minority enrollments. The trend data on minority enrollments, although sparse (especially for Chicanos, Puerto Ricans, and American Indians), warrant the following conclusions:

- Between 1970 and 1977, Blacks were much less likely to drop out of high school than previously, while Whites, especially 16- and 17-year-olds, were more likely to drop out. Nonetheless, attrition prior to completion of secondary school is still about a third higher among Blacks than among Whites.
- Both the absolute numbers of the four minority groups entering two-year and four-year colleges and their proportions among entering freshmen increased between the mid 1960s and the mid 1970s; the proportions have since stabilized at about 12–13 percent.
- The proportion of Blacks in the 25–29 age group who had completed four or more years of college increased from 10 percent in 1970 to 15 percent in 1975. Between 1976 and 1979, the proportion of Blacks, Chicanos, and Puerto Ricans among baccalaureate recipients increased

slightly, while the proportion of American Indians remained relatively stable.

- Between 1973 and 1977, the share of doctorates awarded to members of all four minority groups increased substantially, from 3.8 percent to 6.3 percent. Since 1977, however, the share has declined slightly.
- In the late 1960s, students from the four minority groups constituted only about 3 percent of first-year medical school enrollments; by the 1974–75 academic year, they constituted 10 percent. Since that time, the minority proportion of enrollments stabilized at 9 percent.
- The proportions of the four minorities among total law school enrollments increased from about 3.8 percent in the late 1960s to 6.4 percent in the 1976–77 academic year. Since that time, the proportions of Blacks, Chicanos, Puerto Ricans, and American Indians among law students have changed very little.

In summary, minority representation at all levels of higher education increased substantially between the mid 1960s and the mid 1970s. In more recent years, however, their proportions have stabilized, and few gains have been made since the mid 1970s.

Factors Influencing Educational Progress

Analyses of the two-year (1975–1977) and nine-year (1971–1980) longitudinal samples yielded a wealth of findings, which are summarized here. For simplicity, the results are presented under two major headings: *entering student characteristics* and *college environmental characteristics*.

Entering Student Characteristics

The quality of academic preparation in secondary school is a major factor in the student's academic performance in college and baccalaureate attainment. Academic performance in secondary school, as measured by the student's grade average or class rank, was a much more important predictor of undergraduate grades and persistence than were standardized test scores, although in the case of Blacks, such scores did contribute to the prediction of college grades and persistence.

Study habits and type of high school curriculum were also closely associated with undergraduate grades and persistence. Those students who took a college preparatory curriculum in high school and who entered college with well-developed study skills were more likely to do well academically and to attain the baccalaureate than were those students who took some other type of program (for example, vocational or secretarial) and whose study habits were poor.

As expected, certain family background characteristics indicative of socioeconomic status proved to be related to college grades and persistence. Minority students whose parents were better educated and had higher incomes were likely to perform more successfully than were those whose parents were relatively poor and uneducated. Parental income alone predicts persistence and achievement for all four minority groups but is unrelated to the college performance of Whites. This finding implies that although financial aid (especially grants) has a positive impact on both access and persistence, it cannot compensate for all the negative effects of poverty on the minority student's academic achievement.

In addition, those minority students who gave themselves high self-ratings on academic ability and who were relatively young at the time they entered college tended to make good grades in college and to persist to baccalaureate completion. Among Blacks, scoring high on standardized college admissions tests, feeling well prepared in mathematics, and taking a relatively large number of secondary school courses in science and foreign languages predicted achievement and persistence; among Blacks and Chicanos, attending an integrated high school had positive effects on these outcomes.

College Environmental Factors

The longitudinal analyses examined four general categories of college environmental factors: institutional characteristics, field of study, financial aid, and place of residence.

Institutional Characteristics. Initial enrollment in a community college substantially reduced the student's chances of persisting to baccalaureate completion. This finding, which replicates findings from earlier longitudinal studies, suggests that in those states with hierarchical systems of public higher education—where high school graduates with the best academic records can choose from the full range of postsecondary options, while those with relatively poor academic records are consigned to community colleges— many minority students are in effect being denied an equal educational opportunity.

The quality of the undergraduate college (as measured by such indexes as the institution's prestige, per-student expenditures, and admissions selectivity) was consistently related not only to baccalaureate completion but also to attainment of a doctorate or an advanced professional degree. In short, the higher the quality of the undergraduate institution attended, the greater the minority student's chances of persisting to the baccalaureate and of enrolling in a program of study for the doctorate, medical degree, or law degree. (The only exception to this generalization occurred in the case of American Indians, where the effects of quality measures were mixed.) These findings suggest that one way to increase the number of minority students who successfully complete advanced training is to increase the number who enter the more prestigious and elite institutions as freshmen. Such institutions apparently serve as conduits for students who will eventually go on to graduate and professional schools. These findings have at least two policy implications: first, prestigious institutions should intensify their efforts to recruit more minority students; and second, those institutions in which minority students are now concentrated should be strengthened so that they will be more effective in encouraging their minority undergraduates to enter graduate and professional training.

Field of Study. The student's undergraduate grades are significantly affected by the course of study pursued. Those students, both minority and White, who major in natural science, engineering, and premedical curricula get lower grades than would be expected from their entering characteristics; those who major in the arts and humanities, the social sciences, and education get higher grades than expected. Apparently academic standards in the sciences and engineering are more stringent than those in the other major fields.

During the undergraduate years, there is a substantial loss of minority students who aspire to become physicians, engineers, or lawyers and a concomitant increase in the number who aspire to careers in business and in college teaching. With certain exceptions, these shifts in career plans tend to exacerbate the underrepresentation of minorities in natural sciences and engineering. (It should be noted, however, that White students show similar changes in interests during the undergraduate years.)

Financial Aid. Perhaps the most consistent finding with respect to financial factors is that holding a full-time outside job while in college has unfavorable effects. Minority students who enter college expecting to work full time at an outside job are much less likely to persist to baccalaureate completion than those who enter college with no such expectation. On the other hand, part-time work seems to facilitate persistence, especially if the job is located on campus.

The type of financial aid received is also important. The effects of grants or scholarships are generally positive, but the effects of loans are mixed.

Place of Residence. Students who live away from home while attending college are more likely to persist to baccalaureate completion than those who live at home with their parents; this is especially true for Blacks and Chicanos. The positive effects of the residential experience are consistent with a body of earlier research.*

Views of Minority Educators

The commission's survey of 311 minority educators, whose past experiences and current positions make them a rich resource of information, also contributed to our understanding of factors influencing the educational progress of minorities. Participants in the survey first completed an open-ended instrument asking them to respond freely to questions about facilitators of and barriers to the educational attainment of people from their racial and ethnic backgrounds. Their responses were compiled and categorized to produce a second questionnaire in a forced-choice format. The findings from this second instrument can be summarized as follows:

Asked about factors that facilitated their completion of the baccalaureate, respondents were most likely to mention the encouragement and support of their families and their own educational goals and interests. These factors also motivated their enrollment in graduate or professional school, as did career-related or economic goals and the receipt of financial aid. The chief barriers at both the undergraduate and graduate levels were financial concerns (including problems connected with having to work while in college) and faculty composition and attitudes. In addition, respondents indicated that institutional indifference to minority students was a barrier to their completion of college, and that family responsibilities were often a burden during graduate school.

Despite their high academic attainment (66 percent of the sample of 311 respondents had earned a doctorate, and 26 percent held a master's degree), minority educators feel that they face special problems as professionals. Among the most serious of these problems are the lack of institutional commitment to minorities, difficulty in gaining the acceptance and respect of their colleagues, institutional ethnocentrism that ignores the perspectives and values of other cultures, and being stereotyped and exploited as "minority experts" in ways that limit opportunities for professional advancement. Generally, Blacks were least likely to cite these problems, probably because many of them are employed at historically Black institutions. Another section of the questionnaire asked respondents for their

---

*Astin, 1975; A. W. Astin, *Four Critical Years: Effects of College on Beliefs, Attitudes and Knowledge* (San Francisco: Jossey-Bass, 1977); A. W. Chickering, *Commuting Versus Resident Students: Overcoming Educational Inequities of Living Off Campus* (San Francisco: Jossey-Bass, 1974).

views about obstacles to the educational attainment of young people of their racial and ethnic background. Close to two-thirds cited poor educational preparation. Financial problems were also seen as constituting an obstacle, especially for Chicano and Puerto Rican males. American Indian respondents said that young people of their racial and ethnic background are particularly subject to self-concept and identity problems. In addition, some respondents believed that minority women face problems not encountered by their male counterparts: namely, sex-role stereotypes and conflicts engendered by multiple-role demands.

According to respondents, the barriers encountered by minority students differ somewhat by educational level. Poor teaching and poor educational preparation are major problems at both the elementary and secondary levels. In addition, elementary school children (especially American Indians and Blacks) face barriers related to the home environment (lack of resources in the home, poor health and nutrition, parents who are not able to help their children with schoolwork or who do not become involved in their children's schooling), the lack of effective instructional programs designed to promote cultural awareness and identity and to develop bilingual skills (mentioned most often by Chicano, Puerto Rican, and American Indian respondents), and the lack of transitional instructional programs for students with limited English-language skills (mentioned most often by Puerto Rican respondents). Inadequate academic and career counseling was identified as a particularly serious barrier for minority high school students.

At the undergraduate and graduate levels, financial difficulties loom large, especially for Puerto Ricans. Moreover, poor educational preparation is an obstacle for minority undergraduates, whereas minority students in graduate and professional schools are hindered by the lack of minority faculty, mentors, and role models.

Chicano, American Indian, and Puerto Rican respondents believe that the greatest strength of their young people is strong cultural identity. In addition, Chicanos and American Indians mention strong family and communities as strengths, while Puerto Ricans cite bilingual skills. Blacks, on the other hand, feel that their young people are distinguished most by intelligence, curiosity, resilience, and flexibility.

Asked to indicate what higher education institutions could do to better serve minorities, respondents tended to emphasize these areas of action: the hiring, promotion, and tenuring of minority faculty, counselors, and administrators; the encouragement of college attendance through outreach and recruitment programs to inform students and parents about college benefits, opportunities, and choices; the provision of access through conditional or open admissions; and the improvement of articulation between community and four-year colleges.

Recommendations

Given the current pressure for fiscal stringency, the commission was faced with a critical decision. Would it be more judicious to exercise restraint by selecting and concentrating on just a few recommendations for action, with the hope that cost-conscious government and institutional policy makers would thereby be more willing to consider these recommendations? Or should a broader-based approach be taken?

Several considerations prompted us to choose the second alternative. First, while recognizing that indifference and even hostility to minority concerns has been growing in certain quarters, the commission is strong in its belief that redressing inequality in higher education must become a first-ranked national priority, for both practical and moral reasons. Second, while large financial outlays might be required to implement some of these recommendations, others call for a reexamination of current policies and practices and a restructuring of certain components of the educational system—painful, perhaps, but not expensive. Finally, we welcome the opportunity to address a number of issues that have surfaced in the course of the project and to speak to a number of audiences that have some responsibility for and some interest in making changes. It should be emphasized that many of these suggested changes would benefit not only students from the four minority groups under consideration but all college students, U.S. higher education as a whole, and, ultimately, society at large.

Implementation of the Value-Added Model

The commission recommends:

- That educational institutions revise their testing and grading procedures to reflect and enhance the value-added mission. Such a revision requires, first, that current normative or relativistic measures be replaced by measures that assess the learning and growth of the individual student and, second, that these measures be administered periodically to assess the individual's growth over time. Results from both local and national tests should be routinely fed back to individual students and teachers on an item-by-item basis. Such revised testing and grading procedures will better serve the educational process by providing students, teachers, institutions, and policy makers with feedback on the nature and extent of student learning and growth over time. This feedback will be useful not only in evaluating the effectiveness of educational programs but also in diagnosing the educational progress and needs of individual students.

- That educational institutions use standardized tests for course placement, evaluation, and counseling rather than just for the selection and screening of students.
- That educational institutions enlarge their concept of competency measures to include the assessment of growth in the noncognitive realm: personal development, interpersonal skills, and self-esteem.

Rationale. The principal function of all educational institutions should be to change people: to increase the competence of students, to enhance their personal development, and to help them lead more productive and fulfilling lives. Ideally, testing and grading procedures should be designed to facilitate this value-added mission of institutions.

Typically, testing and grading procedures in higher education are used not to measure student growth or change but to rank students in relation to each other. Because current practices emphasize the screening and certification of students, tests and grades not only fail to contribute to the learning process, but also pose special obstacles to the development of minority students.

Precollegiate Education

The commission recommends:

- That school counselors and teachers make special efforts to assist minority students in understanding the relationship between their education and their future careers and other life options.
- That secondary school counselors and teachers encourage minority students to enroll in college preparatory curricula and to take courses in mathematics, languages, natural science, and social science.
- That schools routinely test new and continuing students, as a basis for undertaking any remedial efforts that may be required to correct for the effects of earlier educational deficiencies.
- That secondary school teachers and administrators, working in close collaboration with faculty from nearby colleges and universities, define those intellectual competencies that are crucial to effective performance in college and develop tests to measure such competencies.
- That such tests be administered on a repeated before-and-after basis to assess student progress and program effectiveness, in accordance with the value-added model.
- That the results of such periodic testing and retesting be a major element in the accountability of school teachers and administrators, and that

those who are demonstrably effective in assisting minority students should be more adequately compensated.

- That the school leadership make greater efforts to ascertain and respond to the concerns of minority parents, to involve them in the operation of the schools, and to assist them in understanding the objectives, procedures, and practices of the schools.
- That the per-student formula now used to allocate resources among public elementary and secondary schools within a school district be revised so that predominantly minority schools receive a greater share of these resources, some of which should be used to develop rigorous academic programs and associated support services for their students.
- That higher education institutions, schools, and departments concerned with the training of elementary and secondary school teachers develop stronger academic programs designed, among other things, to increase the prospective teacher's awareness of and sensitivity to minority cultures and values.

Rationale. A body of research shows that the quality of precollegiate education is critical in determining whether young people go on to college, what kinds of higher education institutions they attend, how they perform in college, and whether they are able to complete their college education. While disagreeing on the causes, most observers agree that in recent years the quality of public schooling at both the elementary and secondary levels has deteriorated, and that the weaknesses of the public education system are borne most heavily by minority students, especially those attending predominantly minority schools located in the inner city and in isolated rural areas. Such schools typically have fewer resources (finances, facilities, high-quality teaching, administrative leadership, community involvement and support) than do middle-class White schools. Moreover, whereas middle-class White students usually have resources and support systems outside the school to compensate for deficiencies in the system, many low-income minority students have no such resources to fall back on.

The consequences of this situation are clear. As data from the project show, high school dropout rates are much higher among minority youth (especially Chicanos, Puerto Ricans, and American Indians) than among White youth. Largely because of their poorer secondary school preparation those minority students who do go on to college are less likely to complete the baccalaureate than are White undergraduates. Moreover, minority students tend to major in education and the social sciences; relatively few choose engineering or the natural sciences as major fields of study.

Community Colleges

The commission recommends:

- That community colleges revitalize their transfer function by establishing as one option a "transfer-college-within-a-college," wherein all students aspiring to a baccalaureate can be brought together and exposed to the same kinds of intensive educational and extracurricular experiences commonly available to students at residential institutions. Funding formulas may have to be revised to strengthen the "college-within-a-college."
- That the transfer program staffs of community colleges work closely with their counterparts at senior institutions to improve articulation.
- That transfer programs within community colleges offer intensive remediation and academic counseling.
- That senior institutions make more effort to facilitate the transfer of community college graduates by setting aside an appropriate amount of financial aid for these students and by offering orientation and counseling to meet their special needs.
- That in areas where senior institutions and community colleges are located close to one another, young people aspiring to a baccalaureate be encouraged to enroll in the senior institution, without prejudice to the continuing opportunity of students in two-year colleges who may wish to transfer to the senior institution.

Rationale. Because they are geographically accessible, relatively inexpensive, and flexible in admissions policies and scheduling, community colleges have opened postsecondary access to many people who otherwise might not have gone beyond high school. Community colleges have succeeded in providing vocational training and adult education for many Americans. The relatively recent American Indian community college movement demonstrates how effective these institutions can be in responding to the immediate needs of that community by offering career associate-degree programs in such areas as range management, animal husbandry, and practical nursing.

Community colleges have been less successful, however, in performing their transfer function. Our data indicate that whereas three in four community college freshmen intend to get the baccalaureate, only one in four actually does so. What makes the attrition problem especially severe is the heavy concentration of minority students in community colleges, particularly in states like California and Texas that have a hierarchical, three-tier system of public higher education Because many minority students do not meet the admissions requirements of four-year institutions, they are forced to enroll in community colleges. For some of these students, the community college's open door leads to a dead end. Moreover, many of those community college entrants who succeed in transferring to a senior institution find themselves as students with advanced standing but without the resources and services that are ordinarily available to entering freshmen—for example, financial aid and orientation.

Academic and Personal Support Services

The commission recommends:

- That colleges and universities strengthen their efforts to help under-prepared minority students improve their study habits and develop their basic skills, by offering tutoring, developmental courses, and academic counseling. Such efforts will not only benefit the individual student but will also help institutions financially by reducing student attrition rates.
- That colleges and universities provide resources to establish centers where minority students can meet together for social and educational exchanges. Such centers can promote a sense of community, can help new students learn about the system, and can foster cultural identity, pride, and strength in such a way that minority students will be able to challenge as well as to enrich and broaden the traditional values of the institution.
- That minority students themselves, as well as local minority communities, be used as a resource in providing leadership and initiatives for the organization of such academic and personal support services, and that they be given a responsible role in decisions concerning the operation and management of minority services.
- That the trustees, administrators, and faculties of colleges and universities give strong and visible support for the development of ethnic studies programs, so that the perspectives added by such programs will be available for the benefit of all students, minority and majority.

Rationale. Data indicate that minority freshmen represent the entire spectrum of academic ability and preparation, but that a substantial proportion enter college lacking good study habits and feeling poorly prepared in reading, writing, and computational skills. Moreover, longitudinal data show that students who lack these skills are less likely to persist in higher education. Both these points are confirmed by respondents to the commission's survey of minority educators, many of whom cited lack of preparation in basic academic skills as a major barrier to educational attainment. Other barriers mentioned frequently were social isolation and loneliness, "culture shock," and institutional ethnocentricity and lack of commitment to minority students.

In recent years, some slight gains have been made through the establishment of ethnic studies—including Afro-American studies, Black studies, Hispanic studies, Chicano studies, Puerto Rican studies, Asian American studies, and Native American studies—on some of the nation's college campuses. Ethnic studies were born out of the campus unrest of the 1960s, when students in general were pressing for more relevant curricula and when minority students in particular were demanding that institutions address their needs. The almost exclusive focus on Western culture and civilization of the traditional liberal arts program was under attack. Minority students complained justifiably that not only was consideration of minority cultures and values absent from the curriculum, but support-service mechanisms were unavailable to them. As a result of these pressures, ethnic studies were introduced in various forms. On some campuses, courses on one or more minority groups are taught under the aegis of existing departments (for example, sociology, anthropology, history, literature). At others, an interdisciplinary major in ethnic studies is offered. At still others, separate departments of ethnic studies have been established. Although the numbers of students graduating with ethnic studies majors is small, these arrangements have the advantage of allowing other students to minor in, or at least sample, such courses and thus to gain some knowledge or awareness of ethnic studies. On some campuses, ethnic studies programs go side by side with an ethnic center, which attempts to address some of the social and personal needs of minority students and faculty in predominantly White institutions. In addition to giving both minority and majority students a new perspective on the total American experience, ethnic studies have contributed to the college community's enriched awareness of minority literature, art, and music. Over the past decade or so, scholarly inquiry into the presence, experience, and contributions of the various minority groups in the United States has produced fruitful results. Nonetheless, ethnic studies still have not gained respectability in the eyes of many academics, and their very survival is now threatened by fiscal exigency and by growing indifference to minority concerns.

The Myth of Equal Access

The commission recommends:

- That educational policy makers and planners revise their traditional concept of equality of access to take into account the type, quality, and resources of the institution entered.

- That the more selective institutions—including the "flagship" (major) universities in each state—review their recruitment and admissions procedures and where necessary revise them to attract and admit more minority students.

- That these selective institutions make clear their commitment to the goal of increasing minority enrollments by providing support services, presenting minority perspectives in the curriculum, and hiring, promoting, and tenuring more minority faculty and administrators.

- That institutions reexamine the educational rationale underlying traditional selective admissions practices. Ideally, the predictive model of admissions should be replaced with a model that focuses on the institution's value-added mission.

- That those institutions using the predictive model of admissions examine the validity of their formulas separately for minorities, with special attention to the possibility that standardized test scores, which pose a far greater handicap to minorities than high school grades, add little to the prediction of college performance.

Rationale. Aggregate statistics on college enrollments mask the fact that minority students are overrepresented in the less selective institutions and underrepresented in the more selective schools—especially the major public universities of most states. Given that the more selective public and private institutions tend to have greater financial resources, more residential facilities, larger libraries, better physical plants, more varied curricula, and more highly trained faculty, it follows that those students who must attend the less selective institutions are denied equal educational opportunities.

Selective admissions based on high school grades and standardized test scores have been justified on the grounds that grades and tests predict college performance. While this predictive model may be appropriate for businesses, it is inappropriate for public higher education, where institutions exist for the benefit of students. Furthermore, the results of our longitudinal analyses show that test scores add little beyond high school grades in predicting the academic performance and persistence of minority students during the undergraduate years.

Financial Aid

The commission recommends:

- That whenever possible students with significant financial need be given aid in the form of grants rather than loans.

- That students be given enough aid so that they do not need to work more than half time.
- That if students are given financial aid in the form of work-study support, it be packaged in such a way that they work less than half time and, whenever possible, at on-campus jobs.
- That federal and state legislators and policy makers support expanded grant and work-study programs.

Rationale. Minority students often start college with heavy financial responsibilities. For example, two-fifths of minority freshmen entering college in the mid 1970s said they had major expenses and debts; close to a third of the Chicano and Puerto Rican freshmen contributed to the support of their parents; and 16 percent of Blacks and Chicanos, as well as 10 percent of Puerto Ricans, were single parents or heads of households. Even though large proportions of these freshmen (90 percent of the Blacks, 83 percent of the Chicanos, 84 percent of the Puerto Ricans, and 59 percent of the American Indians) received financial aid, many of them still had to work at outside jobs. Half the American Indians, a third of the Chicanos and Puerto Ricans, and a fifth of the Blacks worked more than half time while in school. The implication of these two sets of figures is that minority freshmen who do not get financial aid must find outside jobs. Research evidence indicates that working more than half time has a negative effect on persistence, whereas working less than half time, particularly at an on-campus job, has a positive effect. *

Our analyses further indicate that receiving a grant not only contributes to the student's persistence but also gives the student a wider range of institutional options. Finally, the findings with respect to the effects of loans were inconsistent, perhaps because loan programs for college students have changed drastically since the early 1970s.

Bilingualism

The commission recommends:

- That federal and state policy makers examine the goals and outcomes associated with current bilingual education policy and practice, recognizing that no child should be forced to choose between educational opportunity and cultural identity.
- That along with pedagogical considerations, the historical and juridical facts supporting group claims to language rights and cultural continuity

---

* H. S. Astin and P. H. Cross, *Student Financial Aid and Persistence in College* (Los Angeles: Higher Education Research Institute, 1979).

should be kept clearly in view. The right of minorities to establish language and cultural objectives for themselves should be recognized in public policy, and processes should be fostered through which informed and responsible decisions about language and education can be made by the communities concerned.

- That colleges and universities more actively promote the broad-gauged, interdisciplinary, and historically grounded research necessary to inform a more rational, efficacious, and humane national policy concerning language and education.

- That elementary and secondary schools provide the instructional services and resources necessary to maintain and develop the language skills of children who enter school speaking Spanish or an Indian language, if these students or their parents request such services. This recommendation in no way relieves the schools of their responsibility for providing these students with a complete training in English.

- That researchers seek to identify the instructional methods, materials, and programs at both the precollegiate and postsecondary levels that contribute to student performance in school and promote the development of bilingual skills.

- That researchers seek to identify the barriers faced by college students whose command of English is limited as a result of poor instruction in the elementary and secondary schools or of recent migration to this country and to explore ways in which the educational achievement of these students can be facilitated. (The lack of research related to the needs and experiences of bilingual college students frustrated the commission's efforts to understand the dynamics of bilingualism at the postsecondary level.)

- That postsecondary educators recognize their responsibility for and commit themselves to furthering the development of bilingual skills among college students and, through their roles as teacher trainers, support and improve the job training of teachers already working at the elementary and secondary levels.

- That colleges and universities acknowledge and utilize the linguistic talents of bilingual students by providing them with the training and opportunities to work part time on community liaison and on student recruitment and orientation programs; by employing upper-division or graduate students to provide academic tutoring and personal counseling for new bilingual students who need such services; and by hiring and training students as tutors and teaching assistants in foreign language courses and as research assistants on projects concerned with studying language-related issues or with collecting data within bilingual communities. These kinds of opportunities benefit students as well as the institution by enhancing student involvement in the college experience and by providing on-campus employment that is likely to be of greater interest and value than many other work-study jobs.

Rationale. Language is a vital component of personal identity, cultural continuity, and community cohesion for Chicanos, Puerto Ricans, and American Indians. While the commission recognizes that the acquisition of English-language skills is a prerequisite for full and effective participation in most aspects of U.S. life, including higher education, it fails to see why the acquisition of these skills should preclude a parallel acquisition of competency in the language of one's culture and community. Indeed, the commission would endorse the goal of achieving genuine binguality not just for Chicanos, Puerto Ricans, and American Indians, but for all U.S. citizens. The apparently learned disability with languages other than English that affects so many Americans is destructive of cross-cultural and international understanding and relationships.

It is important as well to acknowledge the roots of present language conflicts affecting Indians, Chicanos, and Puerto Ricans. The hostilities with Mexico, Spain, and various American Indian nations generally ended in formal treaties that in almost every case promised to respect these peoples' property, political rights, culture, and language; over the years, however, these peoples have often been exposed to unequal systems of education where English has been imposed as the language of instruction and where native languages have been excluded from the schools. This historical background needs to be kept in view, along with emergent international norms regarding minority language rights, in considering the legal bases for bilingual schooling and other public services in the United States.

Spanish is spoken in and is a vital feature of many U.S. communities and will be for decades to come.* The Hispanics are the fastest growing minority in the country, with an increasing number of dispersed regional concentrations. Substantial migration to the U.S. from Mexico, Puerto Rico, and other Spanish-speaking countries will continue, and the lives of many migrants will be characterized by a complex circulation pattern between the U.S. and their home countries. Survey results indicate very strong support for preserving Spanish and for bilingual education within Chicano and Puerto Rican communities. Knowledge of Spanish provides a concrete link to a rich and creative intellectual and political tradition of worldwide scope

* R. F. Macias, "Choice of Language as Human Right—Public Policy Implications in the United States," in *Ethnoperspectives in Bilingual Education Research: Bilingual Education and Public Policy in the United States* (East Lansing: Bilingual Bicultural Education Programs, Eastern Michigan University, Vol. I, 1979).

and, on a more immediate and practical level, allows people to be active and effective participants in their communities. The demand for young college-trained professionals, business persons, government employees, and service workers with a command of both Spanish and English is steadily growing.

Although an estimated 206 Indian languages and dialects have survived as living languages and a half dozen have 10,000 or more speakers, fifty or so have fewer than ten surviving articulators of the traditions they embody (Medicine, 1979).* Because each Indian language is a product and expression of a distinctive culture, recording and teaching an Indian language represents the preservation and transmission of a whole way of life—a particular mode of viewing and ordering the world and experience. Separated from the living cultures, the languages become essentially meaningless; separated from the languages, the cultures cannot long survive in depth. Thus Indian communities have repeatedly urged that their languages be taught in the schools and that the traditional mechanisms of transmitting these languages be revitalized where they have broken down. Indians in the United States today stand poised before the prospect of a new era in which a recovery of sovereignty and self-determination may be coupled with the command of resources that have the potential to put great wealth in the hands of some tribal governments. The opportunity and need to come to grips creatively with problems of education and language have never been greater.

Federal support for bilingual education dates from the late 1960s and addresses only the most elemental problem of an officially monolingual but linguistically diverse society: how to teach children who enter school with little or no knowledge of English. The Bilingual Education Act (1967) and subsequent state statutes allowed such children to receive instruction in their own language for a transitional period. Thus Spanish and Indian languages are permitted in the schools, but only as a means of facilitating the first steps toward learning English. The child who is proficient in a language other than English, but not in English, is summarily labeled as "language deficient." By 1980 nearly a billion dollars had been spent on remedial and compensatory programs that narrowly define eligibility for bilingual instructional services and seek to return students to regular classrooms as rapidly as possible.

The commission recognizes that government and school provisions for bilingual education, even in their most rudimentary form, are highly controversial, and that there are divisions of opinion about them within the

* B. Medicine, "Bilingual Education and Public Policy: The Cases of the American Indians," in *Ethnoperspectives in Bilingual Education Research: Bilingual Education and Public Policy in the United States* (East Lansing: Bilingual Bicultural Education Programs, Eastern Michigan University, Vol. I, 1979).

Spanish-speaking and Indian communities. It does not pretend to have greater insight into the best resolution of this controversy, nor does it recommend enforced bilinguality for students from these communities. It wishes to affirm its opinion that bilingualism is a strength, and that students who enter the nation's schools speaking some language other than English bring a talent to be developed, not a disability to be overcome. As stated in their value premises, the commission firmly believes that full access to and participation in education and in U.S. social and economic life is an incontestable right of each of these groups, and that exercising this right should under no circumstances require individuals to surrender their cultural distinctiveness, including language.

Graduate and Professional Education

The commission recommends:

- That federal, state, and institutional policy makers increase financial aid for minority students at the graduate and professional levels. In particular, every effort should be made to expand the number of assistantships available to minority graduate students, since this form of aid seems to intensify student involvement in graduate study, promote professional development, and strengthen the bond between student and faculty mentor.
- That federal, state, and private agencies consider implementing challenge grant programs, since such programs seem likely to increase the amount of financial aid available for minority graduate students as well as to strengthen institutional commitment to the goal of increasing minority enrollments.
- That graduate faculties be more sensitive and responsive to the need of minority graduate students to have more freedom and support in selecting research topics, choosing methodologies, analyzing data, and interpreting results, consistent with graduate standards.
- That graduate and professional schools make special efforts to increase their pools of minority graduate students and the presence of minority members on their faculties.
- That federal and state policy makers give increased attention to the nation's long-term needs for highly skilled academic, research, and technical workers. We believe that recent cuts in funding for advanced training programs based on actual or presumed short-term surpluses of personnel in certain fields are short-sighted, and that they disproportionately and unfairly reduce the opportunities of emerging minority scholars to contribute to the general good.

Rationale. Advanced education is an important route to positions of leadership in U.S. society. Despite some gains in the past decade, minority enrollments in graduate and professional schools remain low, lagging behind minority undergraduate enrollments and falling far short of White enrollments at the graduate and professional levels.

Data from the current project contribute to our understanding of the problems confronting minority students who pursue advanced degrees. Five factors were found to affect minority access to, participation in, and satisfaction with graduate and professional education.

First, financial aid is terribly important to minority graduate students and has become a critical issue because of declines in federal and private financial support in recent years. Our analyses revealed that financial aid facilitates entry to and persistence in graduate school. Respondents to the commission's survey of minority educators identified financial concerns as a major obstacle to graduate school attendance. A large proportion of the Ford Fellows said that receiving the fellowship award enabled them to attend the graduate schools of their choice and to stay in school once they had enrolled. The 1980 follow-up of 1971 freshmen indicated that minority respondents who had attended graduate school were far less satisfied with the financial aid counseling they had received than were their White counterparts. Almost as important as the availability of financial aid was its form. Teaching, administrative, and research assistantships that promote professional development are preferable to loans, which do little to encourage students to participate in the apprenticeship that is such an important aspect of the graduate experience.

A second important factor is the type of undergraduate institution attended. Analyses of the 1971–1980 data indicated that the minority student who completes the baccalaureate at a high-quality (that is, selective, prestigious, affluent) college has a much better chance of enrolling in and completing graduate and professional study than the minority student who attends a low-quality college.

Third, the environment of the graduate institution has a major impact on the minority student's participation in and satisfaction with graduate education. Survey respondents indicated that they were often uncomfortable with the cool, somewhat alien, environments of academic departments and research universities. Low minority enrollments and lack of institutional concern for minority students contributed to their sense of isolation and impeded their adjustment. A number of Ford Fellows commented that the inhospitable atmosphere of academic institutions, along with the prospect of taking a low-paying faculty position, contributed to their decision to seek employment in the private sector rather than in academe following degree completion.

Fourth, faculty expectations and attitudes constitute a significant part of the graduate and professional experience of minority students. A large proportion of the Ford Fellows and of the minority educators said that they entered graduate programs feeling stigmatized by their race and ethnicity; minority respondents felt that faculty members all too often assumed that they had been admitted to satisfy affirmative action requirements and that they were less competent than White graduate students. The continual need to prove themselves angered them and contributed to their dissatisfaction with graduate study.

Finally, survey respondents and Ford Fellows reported that majority faculty often failed to acknowledge, let alone support, minority-oriented research interests and associated cultural values. As graduate students they faced constraints in their choices of research subjects and approaches and in drawing implications from their studies, because of negative attitudes, very specialized concerns, and methodological rigidity on the part of faculty. These sources of conflict contributed to the sense of alienation pervading these accounts of the graduate experience.

Minority Faculty and Administrators

The commission recommends:

- That colleges and universities seek to recruit and hire more minority faculty members, administrators, and student services personnel and make every effort to promote and tenure minority educators. Actions do indeed speak louder than words: no amount of rhetorical commitment to the principles of equal opportunity, affirmative action, and pluralism can compensate for or justify the current degree of minority underrepresentation among faculty, administrators, staff members, and students in higher education.
- That top administrators demonstrate their clear and unequivocal support of efforts to recruit, hire, promote, and tenure minorities. In many respects, the administration establishes the campus atmosphere or "tone." Thus, a visible personal commitment to change on the part of one or two senior officials can be critical in effecting increased minority representation on a campus.
- That colleges and universities make every effort to ensure that minority faculty members, administrators, and student personnel workers are represented in all types of positions at all levels within the institution. An unfortunate side effect of the effort to provide better services to minority students has been the creation of positions that are perceived and labeled as "minority" positions; often, minority staff are hired for part-time, short-term, nontenure-track jobs that are supported by "soft" funds from

outside the institution's line-item budget. Because they are isolated from the institutional mainstream, the incumbents of such jobs have little opportunity to influence institutional policies and practices, limited interaction with majority students, and few prospects for advancement.

- That colleges and universities revise their hiring and promotion criteria so as to recognize and reward a wider variety of accomplishments and types of service. Although we are certainly not the first to advocate change in the current review and promotion system, continued adherence to narrowly defined criteria tends to penalize minority staff members who, in trying to fulfill the multiple roles demanded of them, often have little time or energy left to devote to scholarly research and other traditional functions. Institutions that emphasize scholarly activity as a major criterion for promotion should consider establishing a junior faculty research leave program for those young faculty members who have taken on special advising and counseling duties.

- That state legislatures and state boards support administrative internship programs (such as the current state-funded program in the University of California and California State University and College systems) to develop and promote minority and women administrators in public colleges and universities.

Rationale. The commission's survey of 311 minority educators asked respondents to indicate what higher education institutions could do to better serve minority students. The most frequently endorsed recommendation was: hire, promote, and tenure minority faculty members, administrators, and counselors. We believe that this response reflects a recognition of the important functions that minority academics serve as role models; as advisors; as student advocates; as monitors of institutional policies and practices; as dedicated educators committed to educational excellence and equity; as scholars approaching traditional subjects and research questions with new perspectives or laying the intellectual foundations in emerging fields of inquiry; as ambassadors to the minority communities; and, in many cases, as newcomers unwilling to accept the status quo at face value. We also believe that their ranks are thin in number and junior in status and that the foothold they have gained in academe is threatened by institutional retrenchment, the "tenuring-in" of academe, union protectionism of seniority, and rising political, social, and economic conservatism.

In 1976, the National Center for Education Statistics reported that 92 percent of all full-time faculty and 95 percent of full-time faculty at the rank of professor were White. Just over a fourth (27 percent) of the White full-time faculty hold positions below the rank of assistant professor (for example, instructor, lecturer), compared with 44 percent of Black and Indian educators and 41 percent of Hispanic educators. According to recent survey results reported by Florence Ladd, minorities are dramatically underrepresented among college and university presidents, executive vice presidents, and academic deans of predominantly White institutions.*

Government Programs

The commission recommends:

- That the federal government continue to play its leadership role in emphasizing access to higher education for all segments of society. In particular, federal programs in the areas of student aid, institutional support, and special interventions deserve continued support.
- That state and local policy makers, planners, and educators devote more attention to the factors that impede full minority participation in higher education. Federal funding should supplement, not supplant, state and local efforts to support a range of programs and interventions responsive to the needs of minority students.

Rationale. During the past fifteen years, the federal government has assumed major responsibility for the educational equity issues often overlooked by state and local governments. Evidence indicates that federal leadership in this area has contributed to increased minority participation in higher education, and that federal categorical programs—financial aid, institutional aid, and special interventions—have helped to move the higher education system somewhat closer to the goal of equal access.

The success of federal efforts often depends upon the willingness of state and local officials to administer and implement federally funded programs. Unfortunately, state and local performance has not always been consistent with federal priorities, and this discrepancy has had important consequences for minority groups. Local, state, and federal governments have a collective and equal responsibility for minority participation in higher education—a responsibility that does not diminish during times of fiscal stringency.

Minority Women

The commission recommends:

- That colleges and universities provide counseling services and personal support groups to assist minority women in overcoming the barriers that result from double standards and sex-role stereotypes.

* F. C. Ladd, "Getting Minority-Group Membership Top College Jobs," *Chronicle of Higher Education,* May 18, 1981.

- That colleges and universities provide science and mathematics clinics and special courses to help minority women make up for deficiencies in preparation in these subjects, so that these women will be able to consider a wider range of careers. These efforts should be additional to particular interventions at the precollege level.
- That institutions hire and promote more minority women as faculty, administrators, and staff.
- That institutions provide child care services on campus.
- That institutions make an effort to involve those minority women who live at home more fully in campus life—for example, by providing dormitory space or other facilities where these women can spend time interacting with other students.

Rationale. Sex differences in the choice of major field and in career aspirations transcend racial and ethnic differences, but in some instances, are more pronounced among minorities than among Whites. At all degree levels, women are more likely to major in allied health fields, the arts and humanities, and education, whereas men are more likely to major in business, engineering, the physical sciences, and mathematics. Further, although women tend to make better high school grades than men do, more female than male freshmen—and especially minority female freshmen—express a need for special remedial assistance in science and mathematics. Data on earned degrees indicate that minority women are even more poorly represented than White women among those receiving degrees in engineering, physical sciences, and mathematics.

Minority women are heavily concentrated in the field of education. In 1975–76, 8 percent of White women receiving baccalaureates were education majors, in contrast to 24 percent of Hispanic women, 31 percent of Black women, and 32 percent of American Indian women. At the master's level in 1978–79, half of the White women (52 percent) and the Hispanic women (53 percent), 57 percent of the Indian women, and 66 percent of the Black women received their degrees in education. At the doctorate level, about a third of the White and Hispanic women, half of the Indian women, and two-fifths of the Black women earned their degrees in education. Clearly, if minority women are to have access to a wider range of positions and occupations, their current patterns with respect to undergraduate majors must change.

Finally, responses to the survey of minority educators indicate that minority women suffer from sex-role stereotypes and conflicts engendered by multiple-role demands.

Data Pertaining to Minorities

The commission recommends:

- That all federal, state, and other agencies concerned with collecting and reporting data on minorities replace the "Hispanic" category with specific categories that separately identify Chicanos, Puerto Ricans, and other Hispanic groups.
- That, wherever possible, data on Puerto Ricans residing in the United States be reported independently of data on those whose homes are in Puerto Rico.
- That since the designation "American Indian" is ambiguous, and since survey respondents who identify themselves in this way frequently change their response on subsequent surveys, persons who indicate that they are American Indians be asked for further specific information— that is, to specify their tribe or band.
- That all sample surveys strive to oversample minorities, especially the smaller groups—for example, Chicanos, Puerto Ricans, and American Indians.
- That the U.S. Bureau of the Census hire and train more minority census takers and researchers to develop and administer questionnaires and to analyze and interpret the results of Census Bureau surveys.
- That the officials responsible for public higher education in each state institute a comprehensive data system for tracking and monitoring the flows of minority and nonminority students through the community colleges, baccalaureate-granting institutions, and graduate institutions in the state.

Rationale. The success of any attempt to understand the educational problems of minorities or to develop appropriate remedies for these problems is heavily dependent on the quality of the available data. Most sources of data used in this project were seriously flawed; in certain instances, data pertaining to a given issue were simply not available.

Considering the importance of minority issues in our society and the fact that the special educational problems of minorities are far from solved, the costs of improving the quality of existing data and of filling gaps where additional data need to be collected are trivial. With no or very modest funding, the recommendations listed above could be implemented immediately.

Evaluation of Minority-Oriented Programs

The commission recommends:

- That public and private agencies funding minority-oriented programs require that all proposals for such projects include an evaluation component, and that they earmark a certain fraction of the project funds for such evaluation.

- That funding agencies view the results of evaluation studies as a means of improving and strengthening programs, and that they communicate this view to those involved in operating the programs.

Rationale. Evaluation should be a key component of any minority-oriented program, not only because well-designed evaluative research provides vital feedback to guide both program personnel and funding agencies but also because objective evidence of program efficacy can serve to protect the most effective programs in times of budgetary austerity.

It is an understatement to say that the commission was frequently frustrated by the lack of hard evidence concerning the effectiveness of the many programs that have been undertaken to facilitate the progress of minority students in higher education. While impressionistic and anecdotal evidence supplied by the people responsible for running the programs suggests that many of these programs have been useful, systematic objective evidence on program impact is rarely available.

The commission believes that better data on program outcomes will be helpful to funding agencies as they develop plans for future support of minority-oriented programs. Even more important, it will help program personnel as they strive to improve existing programs and design new ones.

The people responsible for operating minority-oriented programs are often indifferent or resistant to systematic evaluation. These attitudes have some basis in reality. In the first place, program staff generally lack the expertise needed to design and implement evaluative studies. Further, evaluation tends to consume limited resources. And finally, program staff are inclined to view evaluation as a threat because it can generate data that might lead others to conclude that the program is not worthwhile. Considering that program staff are almost by definition committed to the belief that their programs are useful and effective, they see themselves as having little to gain and potentially much to lose from program evaluation.

Unfortunately, these defensive attitudes prevent many funding agencies, as well as program personnel, from viewing evaluation as a potential benefit—a source of information to guide them as they develop and refine their programs and as they strive to develop proposals for new programs. Ongoing evaluations, for example, can be very useful in providing funding agencies with information on such matters as the following: elements of the program that might be expanded or elaborated because they seem to be most effective; elements of the program that seem to be least effective and thus need to be changed or eliminated; types of students who benefit most from the program; unforeseen or unplanned outcomes of the program; and the effectiveness of the program compared with the effectiveness of traditional or standard programs.

Further Research on Minorities

The commission recommends:

- That officials in private and state agencies, as well as in the federal government, give priority to minority-oriented research in allocating their increasingly limited funds. These funding sources should aim to establish a process whereby a broad-based and sustained consultation about information needs and issues in higher education can take place within minority communities. Scholars from these communities should have a leading role in efforts to combine imaginatively the talents and energies present within these communities for the purposes of generating research agenda and priorities, carrying out research, and implementing the action implications flowing from these studies.
- That the following specific topics be given much more thorough study:
  a. factors affecting attrition from secondary school;
  b. the quality of education received in secondary schools with predominantly minority enrollments;
  c. the effectiveness of programs for improving articulation between secondary schools and higher education institutions;
  d. factors affecting minority students' decisions to pursue careers in natural sciences and engineering;
  e. factors affecting minority access to the more prestigious institutions;
  f. factors affecting minority attrition from undergraduate study;
  g. the impact of alternative financial aid programs on the achievement and persistence of minority students;
  h. factors affecting the success of community college students who aspire to the baccalaureate;
  i. the importance of sex differences within minority groups;
  j. ways to develop the talents and skills of adults living in minority communities who have not had prior access to educational opportunities.
- That public and private funding agencies give serious consideration to providing relatively long-term support for programmatic research on minorities. Given the importance of longitudinal research in furthering our understanding of issues related to the higher education of minorities, what is specifically needed is a periodic longitudinal study that will make it possible to monitor the flows of minorities through the educational

system and into the workforce, to evaluate the impact of special minority-oriented programs, and to identify educational policies or practices that facilitate or inhibit minority progress through the system. Such a study should begin during the secondary school years (or at the latest by college entry) and should be replicated on a regular basis at least every four years.

Rationale. These recommendations are based on the commission's understanding of prior research efforts as well as on its direct experience in conducting research for this project. They are meant to complement the recommendations regarding data and evaluation. Given the current efforts to reduce federal support for research in education and in the social and behavioral sciences, pressures for funding further research on minority education will fall heavily on private and state agencies.

Response by Kenneth H. Ashworth

In these times of growing specialization and special interests, a person has to be downright brash to dare to say anything at all about anything. Furthermore, when a person comments on a subject such as the higher education of minorities in ten pages he risks being presumed to have said everything he knows, feels, and believes about the topic. How about all the things he leaves unsaid—is he ignorant of those? Unconcerned? What must we assume about his views from such a limited statement? This is especially difficult when the report he is charged to critique has already claimed all of the high ground. Clarence Darrow, in a similar situation, said that the only sensible thing would be to talk about another topic, which he thereupon set out to do. This would probably not be acceptable form here.

I could reduce the risk of being misunderstood or seeming insensitive to minority sensibilities by not providing a true critique. But that was my assignment, and I will proceed with it.

Let me start with a general observation. A major portion of the report is an eloquent statement of the needs for raising the competencies and preparation of more minority students, for reducing obstacles to accessibility and opportunity, and for increasing minority student motivation and understanding of the values of higher education. The other significant part of the report presses for reducing the demands placed on minority students—that is, making accommodations for deficiencies and differences. While the first part is very defensible, highly supportable, and acceptable to most educators and to the public, the second part is less so. Furthermore, a plea for applying less rigorous standards to minorities than to other students is nothing short of patronizing and condescending. For example, the report recommends that promotions of minority faculty and staff members should be made on other bases than those normally followed because the minorities "often have little time or energy left to devote to scholarly research and other traditional functions." If this is meant to be a commentary that all promotions for all faculty should not focus on research and publications, then it should be so stated. As it is, it seems demeaning to minority faculty members.

The report also advocates changing commonly accepted measurements of student competency to recognize such "noncognitive" areas as personal development, interpersonal skills, and self-esteem. Elsewhere the report recommends that minority students should be given more freedom and support in their choice of research topics, methodologies, analyzing data, and interpreting results. Again, this appears to patronize minorities.

Yet another recommendation is to replace current standards of competency, knowledge, understanding, or accomplishment with measures that assess the progress of learning and growth of the individual from wherever he or she starts in college or graduate school. That is, "value-added" measurements should become the primary method of evaluating educational progress. To replace all standards of accomplishment and achievement by measures of relative progress, comparing a student's progress and growth only to himself, is to reject all standards for relativism. If the value-added approach anticipates retaining well-defined exit standards, then the report should say so. It does not say so in its present form.

While the society will likely support efforts to raise all groups to perform effectively against measures of achievement and competency, recommendations for accommodations and changes in the system to excuse or disguise the inability of certain groups to meet the standards of competency will be much less acceptable. Moreover, such recommendations for accommodations can be seized on to substantiate prejudices and reenforce assumptions of nonperformance for all members of the favored minority groups. For example, this report itself states that minorities find that it is presumed that they have been admitted or hired to satisfy affirmative action requirements and that they are assumed to be less competent than whites. There are simply too many whites waiting to judge and find all minorities, whether on the job or in higher education, to be less competent than whites; it is unacceptable for us to play into their hands by advocating that lower standards of competence be applied to minorities. The giving away of credentials and the open advocacy of subjecting minorities to less rigorous expectations is a real disservice to minority students, particularly those who meet all of the same rigorous requirements being met by their white colleagues. Education is not a gift bestowed on individuals; it can only be acquired. Harold Stoke, who was president of Louisiana State University, once said that it is important for the student to understand that trying hard is no substitute for success, that the mastery of knowledge has little to do with the likes and dislikes of the learner, and that generous teachers cannot excuse the student from the requirements that competence demands.

Several recommendations in the report are particularly noteworthy. It is essential that institutions of higher education develop ways to communicate more accurately and earlier to high school students what skills, talents, attitudes, and habits will be most useful for them to be successful in college. In this regard, the report's identification of deficiencies in reading, writing, and computational skills is critical. However, many educators and many successful minority leaders believe that reading is the most fundamental of these. Failure to learn to read effectively in the first five or six years of school will cripple any student for any educational work thereafter. Consequently, merely informing students in high school of what will help them most in college may come too late if adequate work has not been done on reading in the earliest years.

The recommendation that outreach and recruitment programs are needed with parents and students to encourage college attendance is also of major importance. However, another key person in the leaky pipeline is the high school counselor. Often the minority student's counselor, even when he or she is a minority as well, underestimates the capability of the student and discourages him or her from applying to major universities or those with reputations for being rigorous in their requirements. The outreach and recruitment programs need to focus on counselors as well as on students and parents.

The report reveals very clearly where society needs to make its major efforts to increase minority college enrollments—in high school and the pre-high-school years. The data of the report indicate that with the exception of American Indians the other minority students who do complete high school enter college at about the same rate as whites. Consequently, unless the base of minority students graduating from high school is increased, the cohort numbers and percentages for each minority group cannot be raised without inordinately heavy concentrations of effort and attention on the smaller base of minority high school graduates. The greatest results in increasing minority performance at all levels in higher education would come from increasing the pool of minority high school graduates. This data from the report should show the public where it can have its greatest effect in expenditure of efforts and funds.

The report unfortunately seems clearly critical of community colleges—whether intended or not. The outstanding contribution of community colleges to increasing educational opportunities and advancing minority students educationally is apparently deprecated by the report. This may be in part due to a misunderstanding of the role of community colleges. The report says, for example, that regardless of race and ethnicity, community college students are substantially less likely than entrants to four-year colleges to complete four undergraduate years. Although the report does not say so, the analysis apparently did not include all college students enrolled in terminal, technical-vocational programs lasting two years or less.

While it is important to assist junior college students to move on to senior colleges and to increase the baccalaureate graduation rate for minorities, the report nonetheless does seem unduly critical of the fact that minority students tend to take advantage of the educational opportunities of community colleges. The misunderstanding of community colleges' role is further shown in the statement, "Initial enrollment in a community college substantially reduced the student's chances of persisting to baccalaureate completion." This is like saying that people who get on planes to Atlanta arrive in New York less frequently than those who get on planes destined for New York. The report leaves no doubt about its criticism, though, when it says: "Many minority students are in effect being denied an equal educational opportunity" because they go to junior colleges. The report says that "those with relatively poor academic records are *consigned* [italics mine] to community colleges." This implies that adult minority students exercising opportunities for self-improvement are not acting freely, but are in fact being controlled or sorted in some way by someone in society. Furthermore, this view, in effect, ignores the value of community colleges in providing the remedial and compensatory work necessary to assist many poorly qualified students to continue on beyond the community college.

In sum, the report not only does not recognize the efforts of local taxpayers and states to create additional opportunities for education of minorities, it adds insult to injury by implying that the community colleges have been detrimental to the educational welfare of minorities. However, my defense of the significant contribution of the community colleges to minority improvement means that I believe that the proper place for minorities is in the community colleges. They are helping minorities, and we should be willing to recognize that.

The comments of the report on ethnic programs may be overstated. Increasingly, minority students are turning away from ethnic studies programs because they are finding them impractical in terms of employment and even graduate studies. It is not merely the "fiscal exigency" and "growing indifference to minority concerns" that are causing declines in ethnic study programs. To some extent it is outright minority disenchantment. Before additional resources are channeled into such programs and more minority students consigned to them, a careful and objective nationwide study should be conducted to assess why they are declining and whether minorities see them as a means for upward mobility or personal enhancement. Certainly such a study should be made before the decline of ethnic studies programs is used as evidence that such programs are being phased out in order to get rid of minority faculty members.

The report may have discovered at least one thing that most of us have long known about higher education and labeled it as being exclusively a problem of minorities. Minority students' problems with research projects and approaches are described as caused by "negative attitudes, very specialized concerns, and methodological rigidity on the part of faculty." Moreover, the report finds that minority students are "often uncomfortable with the cool, somewhat alien, environments of academic departments and research universities." The report further finds that minorities are turning away from graduate education due to the "inhospitable atmosphere of academic institutions, along with the prospect of taking a low-paying faculty position." It seems the minorities have joined the majority in their views on graduate faculties and that they are no less able than whites to assess future job prospects. While we must acknowledge that minority students may have exceptional problems with these feelings about the graduate environment, we should not forget that these conditions are not unique to minorities.

There is at least one statistical analysis that might be looked at somewhat differently. The report finds that just over a fourth of the white full-time faculty holds positions below the rank of assistant professor, whereas 44 percent of the black and Indian educators and 41 percent of the Hispanic educators hold positions below assistant professor. If we recognize that minorities have only recently begun to be hired in significant numbers because they have only recently begun to acquire doctorates in significant numbers, we should expect them to show up first at the entry level. Consequently, we could expect to find concentrations at that level and should be encouraged that minorities are, at last, being hired—at whatever level. Perhaps the more serious related problem is that in these times of reduced hiring and constraints on funding, minorities with newly earned doctorates are facing the inability of universities to hire and retain new faculty members. The true test will be in examining these same data in another five or six years. Will the minorities have been able to advance in rank?

Of course, hiring and retaining faculty members relates to the key point of budgetary anxiety recognized in the report. Budget cuts are tied to enrollment declines, growing public skepticism of the value of higher education, and both public and private concerns about the cost–benefit relationship of higher education. Taken in a broader context, the "baby bust" will have both immediate and long-term effects deleterious to higher education. Studies by the Office of Manpower Planning and Budgeting have identified even worse problems ahead for the nation and higher education. A major problem in the next century will be the allocation of funds between generations, which does not augur well for higher education. Beneficiaries of veterans' assistance will grow from 4 million around 1985 to 14 million by the year 2000, including surviving spouses. The entire population of the country in 40 years will have the same proportion of people age 65 as Florida has today—16 percent. Health costs, tied to aging, will grow astronomically. The federal noncapitalized retirement systems, such as the civil service system and social security, and many local and state retirement programs as well, will have to be financed out of annual tax revenues. Federal outlays for retirement and disability payments alone will increase from 29 percent of the federal budget in 1980 to over 40 percent in the next 40 years. The dependency ratio, due to the baby bust, will double, so the working generation will have to support the retired generation plus the generation in public schools and colleges. The good news is that we will live longer; the bad news is that most of us are not going to like it. The impact on higher education may be devastating. Budget planners are already looking at how to reduce higher education financing to transfer funds to the other areas. Consequently, the finding of the report that "Many of the problems of minority education are probably beyond the control of higher education" is a gross understatement.

I would like to cite one example substantiating the finding of the report that "higher education is clearly one of the main routes whereby individuals can attain positions of economic and political power." In 1969, when the state of Texas was considering closing the Texas Southern University Law School to eliminate "separate but equal facilities," Dean Kenneth Tollett testified as follows:

> All we are trying to do is to train more black lawyers; train more lawyers from disadvantaged backgrounds . . . because of the predominant role lawyers are playing in the development of this country. The founding fathers at the Constitutional Convention, as you know, were made up of a large number of lawyers; lawyers have always exercised great influence in decision-making processes in this country. . . . If a proportionate number of black lawyers are not trained, then a different kind of thinking will come into play in the decision making in our society and, for this reason, it is so strongly urged that in whatever way possible more black lawyers must be trained if this country is to continue to be governed by the principle of law and order.

At that time, another person testifying was Craig Washington, a student assistant to Tollett. Washington, a TSU Law School graduate, has in recent years been recognized as one of the most outstanding legislators in Texas and is currently running unopposed in Houston for the State Senate. It would be difficult to find a better example supporting Tollett's testimony.

The final report of the Commission on the Higher Education of Minorities is a significant and extremely useful document for those of us working on national and state policies in higher education. The report tells us where many of the pressure points are and where we can find leverage to increase, among minorities, college attendance, graduation, professional and graduate studies, and the hiring of minority faculty members and administrators. The report helps us to recognize the double burden placed on many minority students and faculty members—they are expected to be experts in the fields of specialization they set out to master and also experts in the history, culture, and causes of their minority groups. It helps us to recognize further the double alienation a student may face on campus and at home. The student may feel alienated on campus and may also be discouraged by a sense that education is alienating him or her from family and neighbors. We need to be aware of the shifting external pressures and of the mixtures

145

of feelings possible: envy of progress, success, and material gains and guilt for not doing more to help one's own people. (See Roger Wilkins in April 1982 *Harper's*.) We must be sympathetic to these conflicts and dual pressures on some minority students.

A critique is not an apologia. Therefore, this response is skewed toward the critical. I would rather have used the space to commend and support the far greater positive elements of the report than to nit-pick the few items I could, after great labor, find to criticize.

Recently, the Southern Regional Education Board held a conference on the problems of quality in elementary and secondary education. They were so overwhelming that they were extremely discouraging and the situation seemingly hopeless. The advice at that conference to everyone was that it is important to do *something*—almost anything is better than doing nothing. As there are so many useful things to be done we were urged to pick one or two and go home and do something about them. The Commission's report does the same for us. It leaves none of us with any excuse for not knowing what we might effectively undertake to improve the higher learning of minorities.

The Conference Process: The Human Dimension

Donald Henderson

When Conrad Jones talked me into coming to this conference, he promised me that I would not have to work. "You can sit in on the presentations of the invited papers as you choose. There will be simultaneous discussion sessions which you can visit at your leisure and participate in as you see fit," he said. "You wouldn't mind if I, and the others who planned this conference, rap to you about your perceptions of what's going on, would you?" he asked.

I replied, "No, man, we're going to be talking about what's happening over drinks and dinner and stuff like that, anyway. I'd be glad to rap about what I think is happening. I'd do it even if you didn't ask me."

"Great," was his response. He also chuckled.

When I arrived, Al Moyé and Conrad buttonholed me and talked me into providing the entire conference with my perceptions of what happened, in this last session of the conference. "You're going to be checking things out and rapping to us about them anyhow, from time to time," said Conrad, chuckling—again. So, if some of you have been wondering what I was up to over the past few days—asking all sorts of questions about your perceptions of what was going on and how you felt about it, while frantically scribbling notes about your remarks and those of the speakers and the commentators—I can now tell you that I was preparing for this session and "spying"—that is to say, checking things out for Conrad.

I'm delighted that I did what he told me to do. I've never had an opportunity to be both detached and involved at one of these affairs. I have played the role of monitor, evaluator, critic, judge, prosecutor, defender, and some others I won't mention. It has been great fun, and I have truly enjoyed this conference. I take this opportunity to thank Conrad and his colleagues on the committee for permitting me to be involved this way.

Now to my overview of the conference. My overall impression is that we have had an enormously successful conference. I commend the planners, the participants, and the sponsors. I also heartily applaud the Wingspread staff for the way it has graciously and effectively facilitated and supported our efforts.

The conference has been an unqualified success because, through the interaction of its participants in its several planned activities, it realized its purpose. Moreover, in realizing its purpose, the conference enabled an assemblage of people with more-or-less common interests to become a like-minded group with a common purpose and unified interests. This was accomplished without political, ideological, intellectual, or philosophical rancor. That's no mean feat, given the tremendous potential for rancor intrinsic in many of the issues addressed in this conference. I am so impressed by this that I think this group should get together again and continue its efforts.

I believe that many new and probably lasting friendships have been developed here. We've learned from each other and thereby broadened ourselves, to our own personal and professional benefit. The conference has occasioned these happenings, and I accept them as further indicators of its success.

The conference statement that was produced through these efforts is an additional indicator of the conference's success. It notes, among other things, the need for this society to properly educate all its young people for the ultimate good of the society. It reaffirms that such education should not be compromised because of race or ethnicity—or through economic or social circumstances. Its recommendations are informed, straightforward, reasonable, and proper. In short, this was a very, very good conference. I'd like to share with you my notions of why this conference was a good one and how events here occasioned the development of that like-minded group I referred to earlier.

Conrad and his pals, the executive committee that planned the conference, are very smart, resourceful, purposeful, enterprising, informed, thorough, dedicated people. They designed this conference, selected the topics and the speakers, selected the other participants, and secured this wonderful facility. Their informed choices of participants brought together a remarkable collection of people for 3½ days of discussion and work. The formal events of the conference, now that I look back on them, proved to have been well chosen. They were provocative, and at least one could be labeled "hot." They stimulated a lot of discussion—in the planned sessions and in the unplanned sessions at the bar, during meals, in front of the fireplace, in the halls, and elsewhere. This was a real conference: people were constantly conferring. This collection of able, concerned, and task-oriented people, involved in the formal and informal events, made this conference a remarkable event.

When they selected you, the planners made sure that they got a lot of people with the potential for contributing to the realization of a unified task-oriented group with a common purpose. To do this, they tapped the network—a network that had grown out of the many responsible efforts to provide proper and adequate education for culturally different and under-privileged young people—and with great success, I should add. It's worth noting that each one of us is known rather well by one or more of the people who planned this event. I've learned through observation and in-quiry that the executive committee members are a group of good friends: they like and respect each other and conduct their business in an open and responsible manner. I note this as background for the next observation.

Since each one of us was invited by Conrad or one of his pals (after some discussion and subsequent agreement, I'd bet) we were, in fact, invited by one of our pals. The potential for friendship among an assembly of pals is enormous. The total group was small enough to permit people to get to know each other, but large and diverse enough to permit a thrashing out of dissimilar views and approaches. They stacked the deck—and to good purpose. There are no strangers in the house at this point in the conference. I think that's remarkable.

There we were—this collection of somewhat compatible, potentially friendly, and possibly productive people assembled in this impressive fa-cility ready for something to happen. Let me share with you now my impressions about the coming together of program and people which pro-duced the major events of this conference. By "major events," I don't mean the formal programmed activities. I have in mind the outcome of these activities as reflected in the mood and behavior of the group.

The first such event occurred Tuesday evening. I'm inclined to think the group was more than a little unsettled by some of George Hanford's re-marks. He called our attention to some "unexpected outcomes of increased access to higher education." Important among them were the perception of lower standards to facilitate such access and a relative waste of financial aid given the spotty record of success among these populations. Hanford pointed to the need for a raising of standards for admission, on the one hand, and greater selectivity among the people we seek to help, on the other.

Ripples of unrest rolled across the room in the wake of his remarks. I asked some of you about your perceptions of Hanford's paper and received responses such as "I wonder where he's coming from," and "It sounds like a prelude to closing the door," and "Is he, too, blaming the victim?" And so forth. Hanford's remarks unsettled us. You'll recall that his remarks were preceded by a talk by Stephen Wright, who mentioned the current attempts by the administration to cut funds from existing programs of financial and educational support. Against this background, Hanford's remarks heightened our anxieties.

There was a lot of talk about what Hanford had said, after the session was over. Some of it involved him, although much of it didn't, and we went to bed with it on our minds. At breakfast the following morning, it commanded our attention again—so much so that Edmund Gordon's very thoughtful and provocative paper that morning didn't get the attention it deserved. Fred Humphries' comments following Gordon's presentation focused on Hanford's statements of the evening before, rather than what had gone on in Gordon's session. The formal discussion sessions that followed the presentation had little to do with "undercapitalization" and "underconceptualization," or the ethical and moral considerations undergirding equality of educational opportunity, and the other stimulating concepts raised by Gordon. They centered, rather, on issues of quality and standards, holdover concerns from the night before. When we broke from the session, for example, Sy Purnell and Fred were still pressing George about the need to expand our definitions of quality and excellence.

I think we were on the verge of working through the unsettling effect that Hanford's paper had on us—until the Rosser presentation. Jim Rosser threw the whole place and everybody in it into an uproar. He bluntly stated what we felt to be implied in some of Hanford's remarks. He suggested that many if not most of the programs we sought to sustain were not worth keeping. He noted the low ratio of success in these programs and the exceedingly high rates of attrition over the years. He wondered aloud about the actual competencies of the kids who were successful. He wondered also about the commitment of many of us to quality education for the youngsters with whom we work. He chastised us for not having had the foresight to build our programs inextricably into the fabric of the university, thereby protecting them from the ravages that threaten them at present. He also suggested that part of the blame for our present troubles belonged to the victims—faculty, staff, and students of our programs—for not having taken full advantage of the opportunities we had. He said a lot more, in his very forceful way, than I can recount here. (I note these particular considerations because they're what I saw and heard you reacting to—loud and clear.)

Rosser's remarks caused confusion, consternation, concern, anger, disgust, and some other things among our number. Some of you said you thought he was unnecessarily exaggerating the negative outcomes of our programs while paying no attention to the many very positive outcomes. Some of you also felt he was naive to think that these programs could have been permanently established within a university, no matter what the strategy for doing it. You decried his notion of blaming the victim and expressed dismay about his need to question our commitment. Anyway, everybody jumped all over Rosser.

Whatever you thought of Rosser's paper, the circumstances surrounding his presentation were probably the single most important event of the whole conference. Rosser's remarks had galvanized the conference. He really shook us up. He gave voice to some of our secret anxieties. With his observations, he rallied us to the defense of our programs; with his criticisms, he made us think again about our purposes, our motives, our strategies. He helped us focus our thinking. It was around this event that the conference began to take shape. In jumping on Rosser, the assemblage began to form itself into a group. It began to address the purposes of the conference. Jim listened to the many comments about his paper and promised to make appropriate changes.

Another very important event in the group-formation process was the presentation of Barbara Sizemore. In her calm and deliberate way, Sizemore grounded and stablized us. The results of her research—the data we asked about after listening to Rosser—confirmed our notions that our efforts did make a difference. She described good programs, which, through creative and competent administration and teaching, raised the performance levels of their students phenomenally. Her account of her work in the public schools of Pittsburgh restored our faith in what we were doing. She reminded us that we know more about these matters now and can do a lot more than we could before. She encouraged us not to get hung up on nit-picking our efforts to the point of despair and suggested that we get past responding to Hanford and Rosser and address the work of the conference. We took Sizemore's advice.

Our conversations became animated—sometimes strident but always earnest. We became comfortable with the notion of "value-added" as an indicator of success of our programs. Alex Sherriffs called our attention to data that show that success ratios for regular, marginal, and EOP students are not very different in the California system. He remarked that the value added to the lives of EOP students in this regard is very substantial, indeed.

When Al Moyé challenged Michael Olivas's suggestion that we ought not to align ourselves with business or the military in our efforts to support these programs, most of the group agreed with his challenge. We discovered at that point how alike our thoughts really were. The discussions that evening were spirited; exchanges were serious business. The whole place was active.

The formal presentations the following day were lively, meaty, and provocative. Some of Sandy Astin's data and recommendations generated very productive discussions. But, lively as they were, these presentations were anticlimactic. The group had crystallized. The goals were clear, and the task orientation was in place.

Working sessions were intense that day. The exchange was open, frank, and productive. As I moved from session to session I was impressed by the intensity of effort. Later, when the working groups came together to critique each other's work, the discussion was straightforward and productive. Criticisms and suggestions were listened to, debated, and accepted. Drafts were redrafted and presented again. The next morning that process was completed, and we can now applaud ourselves for a successful conclusion to a valuable conference.

Participants

at the "Policy Conference on Postsecondary Programs
for the Disadvantaged"
Wingspread, June 1982

*Stephen H. Adolphus, Chief
Bureau of Higher Education
  Opportunity Programs
New York State Education
  Department

Robert L. Albright
Vice Chancellor for Student
  Affairs
The University of North Carolina
  at Charlotte

Kenneth Ashworth
Commissioner of Higher
  Education Coordinating Board
Texas College and University
  System

Alexander Astin
President
Higher Education Research
  Institute

Adrienne Y. Bailey
Vice President
Academic Affairs
The College Board

Mary Berry
Commissioner
United States Commission on
  Civil Rights

Herman Branson
President
Lincoln University

*Patrick N. Callan, Director[1]
California Postsecondary
  Education Commission

Ventura C. Castaneda
Assistant Director/Instruction
Department of Educational
  Opportunity
The University of Wisconsin-
  Milwaukee

**Theresa Czapary
Research Assistant/Conference
  Coordinator

---

* Advisory Committee Member
** Staff to Advisory Committee
[1] Did not attend

153

Leonardo de la Garza
Vice President of Academic
    Affairs
Austin Community College

Harold Delaney
Executive Vice President
American Association of State
    Colleges and Universities

Alfredo de los Santos, Jr.
Vice Chancellor for
    Educational Development
Maricopa Community College
    District

*Gilberto de los Santos
Dean of Students and
    Instructional Services
Pan American University

Richard A. Donovan
Director, NETWORKS
Bronx Community College

Vera K. Farris
Vice President for Academic
    Affairs
Kean State College

Robert E. Fullilove, III
Program Officer
Fund for the Improvement of
    Postsecondary Education
United States Department of
    Education

Manuel Gomez
Director
Office of Relations with Schools—
    Educational Opportunity Programs
University of California-Irvine

Edmund Gordon
Professor
Department of Psychology
Yale University

George H. Hanford
President
The College Board

Joseph R. Harris
Dean
Office of Special Programs
City University of New York

Donald M. Henderson
Vice Provost
University of Pittsburgh

Frederick S. Humphries
President
Tennessee State University

*Rupert A. Jemmott
Executive Director
Educational Opportunity Fund
New Jersey Department of
    Higher Education

*Conrad Jones
Assistant Vice President
Office of Affirmative Action
Temple University

Dorothy M. Knoell
Postsecondary Education
    Administrator
California Postsecondary
    Education Commission

Vernon E. Lattin
Associate Vice President
Academic Affairs
University of Wisconsin
    System

Alvin P. Lierheimer
Assistant Commissioner for
    Higher Education Services
New York State Education
    Department

Arnold L. Mitchem
Director of Education
    Opportunity Programs
Marquette University

*Velma Monteiro-Williams[1]
Program Manager
FIPSE/MISIP Program
United States Department of
    Education

*Alfred L. Moyé
Vice President for Academic
    Affairs and Dean of
    Faculties
Roosevelt University

Samuel L. Myers
Executive Director
National Association for Equal
    Opportunity in Higher
    Education

Miguel A. Nevarez
President
Pan American University

Michael A. Olivas
Director
Institute for Higher Education
    Law and Governance
University of Houston

Diane Olsen
Senior Editor
The College Board

Deborah Paruolo
Executive Director
Admissions Referral and
    Information Center

Manuel Perez
Assistant Dean of Student Affairs
California State University at
    Fresno

Silas Purnell
Director
Talent Search Project
Ada S. McKinley Community
    Service

Haskell Rhett
Assistant Chancellor for Student
    Assistance
New Jersey Department of
    Higher Education

James M. Rosser
President
California State University-Los
    Angeles

Alex C. Sherriffs
Vice Chancellor, Academic
    Affairs
California State University

Barbara A. Sizemore
Associate Professor
Department of Black Studies
University of Pittsburgh

Carol F. Stoel
Deputy Director
Fund for the Improvement of
    Postsecondary Education
United States Department of
    Education

Daniel B. Taylor
Senior Vice President
The College Board

Kenneth S. Tollett
Director
Institute for the Study of
    Education Policy
Howard University

Reginald Wilson
Director
Office of Minority Concerns
American Council on
    Education

Stephen Wright
Educational Consultant